Praise for *Holy Fire*

"*Holy Fire* is a great gift—the distilled wisdom of a lifetime of pioneering work on the frontiers of human psychology. Tom Yeomans embraces both ourselves and the wounded Earth in this healing journey. New ways of being and living emerge from this journey that are vastly more satisfying, collaborative and creative. *Holy Fire* is a luminous and penetrating exploration into the "soul-force" that we each bring to this pivotal time in human evolution.

—Duane Elgin (USA), author of *The Living Universe,*
Voluntary Simplicity, Awakening Earth and other books

Tom Yeomans is a pioneering psychotherapist who integrates Roberto Assagioli's Psychosynthesis with Gestalt work and influences from Jung, Tillich, and other major thinkers. *Holy Fire: The Process of Soul Awakening* is his masterwork. This book is essential reading for anyone with a depth concern with transpersonal psychology. It is especially valuable for those grounded in Psychosynthesis, since it provides a creative revisionist view of Assagioli's great contribution. It contains invaluable practice exercises as well as reflections on earth psychology and kosmos psychology. It offers invaluable hints for practitioners. A special treasure are the notes Yeomans kept on Assagioli's personal comments to him. This is a necessary contribution to the literature on human evolution.

—Michael Lerner (USA), Founder, Commonweal, Bolinas CA

Honed from a lifelong career informed by Psychosynthesis and Spiritual Psychology, Dr. Yeomans steps beyond his training and into the direct exploration and cultivation of the Soul. His work is designed to set the Soul alive as a fire on Earth to renew, restore, and show the way ahead, both for the individual and society. The book is a masterful description of the understanding and functioning of the Soul within the context of bio-psycho-socio-spiritual human being. The exercises provided can be used by the individual, or within a therapy or coaching relationship, or for group work.

This seminal work is based on a lifetime of practice, teaching, and training professionals. The practical vision set forth here supports the individual in the essential work of self and soul development, and gradual liberation from the traumatizing defenses acquired during the course of growth and development in a social context unconscious of the Soul. The release of Soul energy through the lessening of these defenses allows each of us to take our place in the greater Whole via the Here and Now. And this experience in turn shapes the necessary decisions, directions, and work needed to make our world supportive of the flowering of Humankind.

—Kathy Sanders M.D., (USA) Psychiatrist, Department of Psychiatry, Massachusetts General Hospital and Harvard Medical School

Holy Fire

THOMAS YEOMANS, PH.D.

Holy Fire

The Process of Soul Awakening

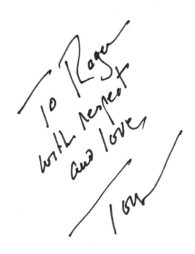

To Roger
with respect
and love

Tom

A CONCORD INSTITUTE PUBLICATION

Printed in the United States of America. First Edition.

ISBN 978-1-7327843-5-2

Paintings by Thomas Yeomans
           Frontpiece *Fiery Earth*
           Back cover *At Home on Earth*
Paintings photographed by Chris Daugherty
Graphics by Scott Smith, Copycat Print Shop, Greenfield, MA
Book design by Maureen Moore, The Booksmyth, Shelburne Falls, MA
Editorial services Ellen Eller, Shelburne Falls, MA

γνῶθι σεαυτόν

—Delphic Oracle

Within us is the soul of the whole, the wise silence,
the universal beauty,
the eternal One

—Ralph Waldo Emerson

We must learn to live as souls on earth

—Roberto Assagioli, M.D.

Other Books by Thomas Yeomans

Prose

The Live Classroom (ed.) (1973)
Psychosynthesis in the Helping Professions (ed.) (1984)
Readings in Psychosynthesis, Volume I (ed.) (1985)
Readings in Psychosynthesis, Volume II (ed.) (1988)
Soul on Earth: Readings in Spiritual Psychology (1999)
Occasional Notes (2006)

Poetry

The Singled Eye: Poems (1985)
For Every Child a Star: A Christmas Story (1986)
The Flesh Made Word: Poems (1990)
On Earth Alive: Poems (2000)

Dedication

To all those who, knowingly, and unknowingly,
seek to awaken and to love.

CONTENTS

FOREWORD

Piero Ferrucci

We often have our best insights under the shower, or driving to work, or peeling potatoes: mundane contexts, when the mesh of our thoughts is a bit less tight, and new ideas have the chance to make their way in. Not so for the author of this book, Thomas Yeomans, and for the realization that dawned on him, later to become a milestone in the narrative of his inner life. Listen to this story.

If you walk into the Church of Santa Maria Novella in Florence, Italy, you notice beautifully crafted golden marks on the floor. They tell you where the sun's rays, focused into a single beam, will hit the floor at midday on each particular astrological month of the year: for instance, Capricorn for the winter solstice, Cancer for the summer solstice. The light comes through an optical device on the façade (the gnomone), and ends its cosmic journey precisely within a small area on the church ground, a spot that varies according to the seasons of the year. The whole church is an astronomical instrument! It situates you in the cosmos and shows you your place under the stars, in the context of all history. What a striking contrast to all those anonymous "non-places" we find in the contemporary world, like supermarkets and parking lots, where you feel like nobody in no man's land.

Years ago, Tom Yeomans, then a 19-year-old young man, visited this church in Florence, and reflected inside it for hours. That left a deep mark in him. I am not surprised that in his book, which represents the pinnacle of his thinking through decades of work in the field of spiritual consultation and education, he sees cosmos as one of the focal experiences in the spiritual, or transpersonal, life. Cosmos (or kosmos, as he prefers, following the Greek origin of the word) means order. Realizing kosmos is about realizing our place on Earth, sensing "our own beauty and the deep order of our life" as well as the beauty of the surrounding universe. This insight is accompanied by a feeling of exquisite harmony.

In his reflection years ago Tom tackled the theme of Jesus Christ's humanness (as he describes in his text), and realized the central place and concrete possibility of the Spirit in human existence. He saw that Jesus Christ is like you and me, that Spirit can be embodied in our day-to-day living. That experience gave direction to his subsequent life and thinking. It is fitting that in this very church you can find a landmark fresco by Masaccio representing the Holy Trinity. This great painter of the early Renaissance was the first to paint Jesus as a human being in flesh and blood, rather than a stylized golden icon, as was common before him. The people Masaccio represented were three-dimensional: they occupied a space like the one in which we spend our everyday life. They were fully human, and so was Jesus Christ. This was a breakthrough that made possible the flourishing of the Renaissance and the new humanism. I do not know how much of this the young Tom Yeomans knew, but surely he could not have chosen a better place for his insight.

I have so far spoken of church and of religion. But religion is just one way of expressing and explaining the unfathomable. Spirituality has gained increasing attention as a legitimate subject of study in the field of psychology—that is, a secular, rigorously empirical view of human experience, not influenced by faith, or belief. This is a crucial development, because spiritual health is an acknowledged component of our wellbeing. The World Health Organization recognized this point in its 2011 statement: "Health is a dynamic state of complete physical, mental, *spiritual* [emphasis added] and social well being and not merely the absence of disease, or infirmity." The numinous, the thirst for transcendence, awe before the cosmic mystery, the expansion of our personal boundaries, a sense of oneness with the All: these and many other experiences may be part of our everyday existence, and can be studied for what they are—phenomena that are highly desirable, nourishing, revelatory, and healing for a great variety of people. Such is the perspective of this book. Yet in reading it we come to see that it is not enough to consider the search for Spirit in human existence. That is not the whole story. The theme here is much stronger than mere recognition of the spiritual dimension's existence alongside other realities. The Self, or Soul, is central. It is the protagonist. It goes through a journey: Soul on Earth, as Tom Yeomans describes it, has a task to fulfill. Soul is not just another beautiful experience, or comforting support. It is the main subject. Ignoring it may lead to all manner of unease and pathology.

Tom Yeomans leads with an ace: a quotation from a session with his (and also my) teacher, Roberto Assagioli, the psychiatrist who created Psychosynthesis. Tom and his wife, Anne, came to Florence in the '70s to study with him for several months, and settled, with their children, in this city. I remember with pleasure the warmth and beauty of their family life when I visited them during that period, the excitement of their new learning, the journey in a new culture and in a new universe. The words Assagioli spoke to Tom are a form of magic. You read them, and they change your perspective, and, if you truly understand this shift, your whole outlook on your own existence changes dramatically. After all, good education and good therapy are just this: shifting your perspective, letting you see the same reality from a different angle. Assagioli says we should not think of ourselves as personalities who have a Soul and yearn for it, who feel the need to go back and rediscover our own true roots. Instead he reverses our usual way of thinking: you already are a Soul; you are a timeless being, free of fear and other worldly constraints, endowed with deep wisdom and immense potential, huge resources of intelligence and love, and a cosmic, not a local, perspective. This being that is you has a project to realize on Earth, during a brief journey on this Planet. It has a task of beauty and love to fulfill. This task has to be worked out in space and time, in our existence, and through a means that we call our personality. Our personality may be seen as a vehicle, a means to expression. Aristotle's concept of entelecheia, and, recently, James Hillman's idea of the soul's code, are along this line.

There is a plan, a pattern to actualize. So the Soul needs to express this pattern through a human personality with all its capacities and shortcomings; a personality that may be distracted by ambition, by the search for pleasure, by fear or anger, or by any of the immense number of factors that conspire to distract us from our journey on Earth. You, the Soul, have a task, and must accomplish it through a vehicle. This vehicle may be ready and in top shape, and the work begins; but it may be opaque, unconscious, disjointed, in which case it needs to be opened, refined, educated, so as to become ready for the job at hand. The personality may, or may not, collaborate, may, or may not, transcend its provincial outlook (compared with the cosmic perspective of the Soul). It may go through detours, it may have severe failings, blocks, tics, prejudices, obsessions, or fears, any of which can veil, or impede, the Soul's enterprise. So the case may also be that the Soul, rather than bravely journeying on Earth, is wearily, heavily slouching on its path, or just wandering with no destination in mind.

This is where education, psychotherapy, and counseling come in, as ways of aiding the Soul in its journey, making it easy, conscious, productive, and happy. Of course, it is never a matter of imposing one's views, or directing someone else's life, but of unboxing: you help people discover what's inside the package. You guide a Soul in the search for its own whereabouts and direction. And you always move within the cosmology of the clients: you do not convert them to yours.

The journey of the Soul on Earth is essentially a happy one—as long as we do not sabotage it. But we do sabotage it—even worse, we lose our Soul—and that causes suffering. Tom Yeomans created the concept of "Soul Wound," which is the loss of our connection with the Soul (a concept also developed by our colleagues John Firman and Ann Gila as "primal wound"). This happens when the early environment of the child, mainly the parents, but not only, does not recognize him, or her, as a Soul. If you are not acknowledged for who you truly are, and instead are consistently seen as something you are not, you will lose contact and confidence in yourself as a Soul, and with it, your knowing, your powers, and your capacity to love. You have no more contact with your cosmic origin and you do not know who you are and what your task is. You are like a traveler lost in a foreign land, ignorant of the trip's purpose, perhaps even that it is a trip. This situation is accompanied by a sense of profound loss, bewilderment, and despair. So the journey of the Soul is not all exhilaration and joy. It may entail effort, doubt, disorientation, and suffering as well.

I find it intriguing that Tom had the insight of Soul Wound in the city of Rotterdam in the Netherlands, while collaborating with Dutch pathologist Marco de Vries. Rotterdam immediately calls to my mind the famous statue in its main square, representing a human figure with a hole instead of the heart (a wide wound made of emptiness) and arms outstretched in despair towards the sky. The statue was originally created by the sculptor Ossip Zadkine to represent his dismay when he returned to Rotterdam at the end of World War II and found a heap of ruins after the bombings of the town center. The statue is a cry of horror, it is the dread of human cruelty and the folly of war, and it is also the empty heart of human beings abandoned by all powers and left to their own misery. What statue could better represent Soul loss?

The role of those who help the Soul come to terms with its destiny is a sacred one, and should be regarded as one of the highest privileges. It deserves to be fulfilled by people who understand its significance, are fully trained for it, and have the best tools at hand. Tom

Yeomans provides various constructs and techniques to make this work effective and meaningful, and his book is extremely useful to all who are learning this art, or are already experienced in it and want to refine it. I was especially interested in the concept of "arenas of experience," specific occasions, or areas, or factors, through which we can better understand the Soul Journey so that it may come to fulfillment. Some of the arenas are, for instance, the body, daily life, death, the spiritual adversary, and the spiritual allies. Take the spiritual ally: it may be an inner image, a historical figure, an idea, a friend, even an animal that supports the Soul in our flourishing. These are all precious ideas to keep in mind as we accompany somebody's "Soul process."

A lot of attention is given also to the pathology of the Spirit. The Soul interacts with our unconscious, and in this way can create all kinds of imbalance and difficulty. *Tantum religio potuit suadere malorum* wrote the Latin poet Lucretius: "To such heights of evil are people driven by religion." Not only religion, I would add, but with all forms of spirituality. This is fertile, but dangerous territory: the Soul transforms and redeems our life, but when improperly managed/dealt with, this process can lead to inner splits, intolerance, fanaticism, sects, psychosis, crusades and witch-hunting. We will be in a better situation if, in approaching spirituality, we use the tools of contemporary psychology as well as plain common sense, as Tom Yeomans does/is doing in his/this book. This subject is of prime importance especially in our frightening and electrifying times.

Moving easily between theoretical outlook and practical guidance, the book offers exercises with step-by-step directions. These are invaluable tools for orienting and supporting serious seekers or anyone who helps people in their spiritual quest. The Appendix is devoted to Notes to Practitioners and Assagioli's aphorisms—phrases that embody a basic teaching, such as: "there is no security, only adventure," "you are perfectly imperfect," "your Soul knows all about it; it is only waiting for you to find out."

We live in a dangerous era full of tensions, disorientation, and upheaval. Tom Yeomans' powerful contribution gives tools we can use to understand the deep reasons for the darkness we are going through, and to emerge from it with new hopes and vistas.

Fiesole, July 2019

PREFACE

I had a dream a few years ago of a vital spark of white fire at the center of every cell of my body—an energetic nucleus that, as it began to flare more brightly, quickened other cell sparks, both within my body and in other people's. Then I saw that this white fire was deeply kindred and resonant with the light of the Universe and the sun-moon-stars, and, as I watched in wonder, an energetic resonance and holy conflagration flared up between the cell sparks in my body and the twinkling of the stars.

I woke with a sense that I had been given a great gift.

—Thomas Yeomans

This book is about human beauty—the deep beauty of the soul as it emerges and shines more and more fully within us. It is about the process by which this emergence comes to be, and the vicissitudes of the journey that we take in order to be fulfilled in this way. It is a report from the 50 years or so of what I have experienced and learned from working with others to support and nourish this soul birth and journey within their lives, and it is also a reflection on my own experience of this birth and journey and the experiences along the way that have led to understanding this process more clearly and deeply.

The title, *Holy Fire,* evokes the experience of sheer vitality and life force that I have come to see as the core of the human soul. It is this white fire, I believe, that we seek to find and express through our lives, knowingly, or unknowingly, and our life journey is the process by which we come into this fiery aliveness. The world both supports and impedes this living process, as we shall see, and so daily life on earth becomes the territory through which we journey to deal with these obstacles and to nourish this fire within us.

This is not a fire that consumes, or destroys, but rather a fire that illumines our experience, and brings to light learning that has been latent and which is needed now. It is a white fire, as in the dream above, that awakens and transforms our consciousness. This fire can seem to come from the outside, and as a result of specific events, but in essence it is arising always from inside us, from every cell of our body and being—a spark of force and vitality that quickens and expands our consciousness and calls us to go deeper into our given life. And it is this fire, I believe, that joins us, within a living Universe, to all other beings.

The subtitle, *The Process of Soul Awakening,* speaks to the view of spiritual awakening and maturation as a process more than a moment of revelation—a gradual dawning in our human consciousness of the true nature of our self and the world. The phrase enables us to differentiate this process of soul awakening into phases, or facets, and to get a better sense of where in the process we are. It also enables us to develop psycho-spiritual practices that can support this process at specific different points, and that are designed to help with the very particular challenges of these different phases. And finally, it places the soul directly within the dynamics of human development and maturation, and posits that the experience of soul is changing within us over the course of a lifetime. This perspective also holds that a task and opportunity we have as humans is "to learn to live as souls on earth," to fully embody and express this holy fire within us, and that this happens gradually by means of a process of soul awakening that can be studied and supported consciously.

I have written *Holy Fire* with the intent to inspire and encourage my fellow human beings to further inquiry and exploration of the human soul and the soul journey we take on earth. I mean the book to give the serious seeker a sense and feel for the territory of the soul and the process of soul awakening. I also hope that the book will give practitioners/professionals practical ways to understand and support this soul process better in their clients as well as in themselves. And, finally, I seek to link this individual soul work to the myriad troubles we have at the moment on the planet as a species, and to present it as one of many means to help heal and transform how we are living on earth now.

At the beginning I must confess that this is a challenging endeavor that puts me at risk of failing to make known clearly enough the ways of the soul. This is because the experience itself is innately ineffable and deeply mysterious, and very private and unique to each person. The soul in no way submits itself to predictable order, or dogma, and it is in essence "wild" in its nature. Further, I have learned over the years that the process of soul awakening is extraordinarily complex, with many dimensions and challenges, and does not yield to under-standing easily. Even hindsight tends to be murky, and rarely do we know clearly where we are going.

Despite this complexity I have also learned that conscious soul process work is worth the effort, and that there are principles and patterns that are reliable. I have seen again and again how this work gradually evokes and strengthens a deeply felt sense of one's unique self as well as a profound experience of intimate connection to others and to All Life—a fruit that is well worth the labor. And I have witnessed again and again how this soul process works, in time, to give birth to the soul's deep beauty and to a holy fire that burns more and more brightly within us.

Holy Fire is not academic in nature. Though it is grounded in decades of professional work and personal experience with the soul, its intent is to inspire and inform more than to instruct those whose interests and concerns are focused on the nature of the soul and the soul journey. I mean it to be more experiential than analytical, and I have written it from the perspective of the practitioner and artist that I have been over these years more than the academician I was trained to be. In this spirit, the book includes my poems and paintings as well as text and diagrams, in order to present multiple perspectives on the soul and our journey of awakening. In Part II I include representative practices that may be useful in doing the details of this soul process work. I also, throughout the book, include experiences from my own life and journey, as they are relevant to the experience of the soul. In this sense, the book is also in part a spiritual autobiography.

You will note that I repeat certain ideas as I move through the book. This is deliberate, for it takes time for this all to sink in, and I find it useful for the ideas to return with new perspectives. The thoughts and experiences, therefore, take the form of a spiral more than a line, and this is both intentional and appropriate, for I have come to see that this is also the way the soul works in us toward our awakening. Also, you will not find footnotes or formal references in the book, nor a bibliography at the end. This is a conscious choice on my part to keep the tone of the writing informal and conversational, for I think this will best support the impact I would like the book to have.

The findings are necessarily incomplete and provisional, as the vicissitudes of this soul journey can never be fully known, and we are only beginning to learn how the human soul "works" in us. They may, however, be useful to others in their search, they have been so to me, and it is in this spirit of continuing exploration that I record them here.

The Beginning

In a way I had no choice but to pursue this course, for this work came to me at age 19 in a church in Florence, Italy, when I was least looking for it, and since that day it has been my personal quest and professional calling. It happened this way.

In July of 1960, at age 19, I was traveling in Italy and found myself one day in Florence in the Church of Santa Maria Novella, across from the railroad station. A question had been arising in me over the last weeks, and it blossomed there. My struggle at that time was with the true nature of Jesus Christ, and the way I formulated it that day was, "If he is an expression of the fully human being, deeply connected to the Divine as well as the earth, then I can model my life after him. If he is half human, half divine, a demi-god, then I cannot." I stayed in the church for hours, while my friends waiting outside thought me a bit mad, needing to know, or to decide, what was true for me. In the end, after much deep reflection, I chose the fully human being, a man like me, and I left the church with the resolve that I would learn to live accordingly. This choice set the course of my life. I recognize it now as a first experience of my soul calling, but at the time I had no idea what had really happened, I only knew this fully human Christ was true for me.

That Fall I returned to college as a junior and enrolled by chance in a two-year course with Rev. Paul Tillich, one of the greatest Protestant theologians of the 20th century, entitled "The Self-interpretation of Man in Western Thought." Each semester was devoted to a different period in Western history—Classical Greece, the Hellenistic Period, the Middle Ages, and the Modern Period. The course was large—700 students—and Professor Tillich lectured from a podium on the topics in a mix of English, German, and Ancient Greek. The breadth and depth of his understanding was marvelous, and with this erudition he built the course around the question for each period of "Who are we? Who is the human being and what are our capacities?" Each era had tried to answer that question, and he presented their responses.

What struck me most was that the response of the Modern Period was, in his mind, not clear yet. In the notes I took the last words I wrote were,

We have no defined telos (Ancient Greek for "outcome," or "end")
yet. Still formulating. We are all in the situation of working and

waiting. Waiting is the highest tension. Maintain yourself 'in spite of' until a telos is found. It takes guts and faith. Embrace insecurity. Stay open. Don't force a premature answer. Don't go back to the old answer. Stay bare and seek.

"Stay bare and seek." This rang so true in my youthful mind, and the course encouraged me deeply to keep going with this question of who we are now in the Modern and post-Modern period and who we can become.

I would arrive at these lectures on a motorcycle, a very cool undergraduate, I thought, yet by the end of each I was often in tears, moved deeply by the quest and the question. I realize now, in retrospect, that the impact of this course on me built on the experience in Florence, but broadened the context from a purely Christian one. In these last years of college I was realizing that this question had been, and was still being asked by philosophers and artists as well as theologians. It was, in fact, clearly a question for all human beings and it stirred me deeply—I would now say, in my soul. The tears, I recognize now, were from the movement of my soul and the calling that was emerging to pursue this question of "who we are and who we can become"— one that would become the core of my personal journey and professional work, though, in truth, I had no idea of this at that time. After these inspiring lectures I merely mounted and rode off on my motorcycle, preferably with a co-ed behind me, and went back to being a cool undergraduate.

A few years after graduation from college a dowager great aunt looked at me with her steely eyes and said, "Tom, I am worried you are becoming a rolling stone." My father, later in life, asked me in some confusion, "Why were you always leaving one profession after another, particularly when you were doing well in each?" A friend and college classmate commented once, shortly after graduation, rolling his eyes, "All those brains and no ambition." It is true that in those years after college I had not yet found what I was looking for and was restless, but it was not true that I had no ambition. It was not for myself, however, but for finding the right ideas to work on. I remember saying to a friend at that time, "I want to work on something that is as common as a can opener, that has universal use for people." For this I had ambition and drive; I just did not know clearly exactly what the question was, nor how to find the form to explore it. It took another ten years before I did.

In my 20s I began to explore this question of "who we are and who we can become," without quite knowing it, in a variety of disciplines. I had majored in Classics, particularly Ancient Greek, in college, and wrote a thesis on the Theban Trilogy of Sophocles—plays that deal deeply with this question of who we are and who we might become. I then studied Philosophy, Politics, and Economics in England the year following graduation. Then, after two years of high school teaching and a year of urban community work, I returned to graduate school where I studied Anthropology for a semester at the University of California, Berkeley, before switching to Comparative Literature and completing a Master's degree in that field. All these experiences were part of the search. I was restless still, however, and finally left Berkeley and took a Ph.D. degree in Humanistic Psychology and Education at the University of California, Santa Barbara, for I had happened by then on Carl Jung and Humanistic Psychology, and particularly the writings of Abraham Maslow and Carl Rogers. I had also discovered the Human Potential Movement that was exploding at that time at the Esalen Institute and other growth centers in North America. At the end of one training weekend in Big Sur I came home to my wife, Anne, and said, as I walked through the door, "I think I have found my work." I was getting closer to having the means I needed to pursue my life question.

While working on the Ph.D., I happened to read Roberto Assagioli's book *Psychosynthesis* and soon after took training in this psychological approach to human development—one that included the soul, or what he termed "the Higher Self." I could feel I was getting closer in my quest, and was excited. At age 30, after my father had long given up on me settling down professionally, I began to work in this "school" of Psychology, Psychosynthesis, set within the larger framework of Existential/ Humanistic/Transpersonal Psychology. I had finally found a means to my end.

I had now chosen Psychology as the way to explore this question, rather than Theology, or Anthropology, or Literature, and for the next 20 years I worked in Psychosynthesis as a therapist, teacher, trainer, and writer. Then, at age 50, I coined the term "Spiritual Psychology," due to some limitations I felt in Psychosynthesis at that time, and continued my quest under this rubric. That same year, 1990, I founded the Concord Institute, in Concord, MA, where we had moved in the '80s, and under its aegis conducted professional training programs in individual and, eventually, group work. I also taught Psychosynthesis and Spiritual Psychology widely throughout North America and Europe, and in the '90s, helped a Dutch colleague found a cancer research institute in Rotterdam, Holland and, with a group of Russian psychologists, co-founded a post-graduate training institute in St. Petersburg, Russia, based on these approaches.

During this middle period of my life my professional work expanded considerably, but it remained always focused on the question of "who we are and who we can become." During this time I also wrote poetry as a way to explore the question and over that time published three books of poems. At age 40 I began to paint as another means of exploration. In my search I also reached back in my own cultural tradition to the writings of Ralph Waldo Emerson and Henry David Thoreau and, touchingly, to the writings of my grandfather, Edward Yeomans Sr., who was, in his own way, as a progressive educator, also concerned with this question of "who we are and who we can become."

Soul Psychology
In all this, the language, principles, and practice of Psychology became the means of exploration, and it is in that language that this

book is written. This choice was possible because of a cultural and intellectual shift during the last decades in the relationship between religion and spirituality such that spiritual experience became seen as possible without religious form to explain, or enhance, it. This meant that the secular discipline of Psychology could be used to support and enhance spiritual experience, and following that, secular professionals could work with this dimension in their patients' and clients' experience.

Carl Jung was a pioneer in this shift in the first half of the 20th century, as was Roberto Assagioli, but by the '60s there were many more who were following suit. Fourth Force Psychology, sometimes termed "Transpersonal Psychology," is an outgrowth of this profound figure/ground shift, and it has allowed me and countless others to work with the soul within a secular existential and experiential context, and to expand our psychological thinking and practices to include this deep dimension of human experience.

Now

My life has been devoted to an exploration of, and response to, this question of "who we are and who we can become." This book holds much that I have learned by following the question into all the places, light and dark, to which it led. I have no idea why it came to me the way it did and became an organizing principle of my life, but it did come and stayed, and gradually I came to recognize it and pursue it more and more consciously and deliberately. *Holy Fire* is a fruit of all that time and effort spent in the company of so many people in so many countries since the '60s who were broadening and deepening the frame of Psychology in this way, and I am forever grateful to them, named and unnamed. Many, many teachers, writers, artists, have helped me along the way, and I make note of them in the text in various ways, and would not be here without them.

At the same time, I am here finally on my own experience and authority as to what I have learned and understand now about this question of the soul and the process of soul awakening. I gladly accept responsibility for this, knowing that you, the reader, will take what is useful and let the rest go. I am amazed and grateful that my life led in these directions, and that I can share what I know now with you. And I hope for years more to continue my quest.

Note that in the book I use particular words because they seem to me to come closest to the experience I am describing, and I use particular ideas and concepts and practices because they seem to me to be most effective in illuminating the mystery of the soul. They are not, however, THE ANSWER, and they may not be at all useful to some. They have been useful to me and that is why I am sharing them. And, of course, I hope they will be found useful to others as well. Time will tell.

Question and Quest

Again, the question that first emerged in the church in Florence and that I was called to pursue for all these years and still ponder is "Who are we essentially as human beings and who can we become?" In Paul Tillich's terms, as I first heard it, it was "What is the self-interpretation of the human being in the modern and now post-modern era?" How do we understand our true nature and how do we best support and nourish this nature to full maturity? Everything in this book is a response to that question and part of a life-long search and journey I have undertaken to see what I could find out. I am so grateful to have been given this quest and question so early in my life and to have followed it out. Now, in my late 70s, I can see that it was indeed mine to live and explore, to "stay bare and seek," and I am deeply grateful for this unexpected gift.

INTRODUCTION

I want now to put forth some basic parameters of my thinking about, and work with, the soul and the process of soul awakening, as a way of introducing the theoretical context of my pursuit of this life question. I will then, in the rest of the book, go into much more detail as to what I have come to understand within these parameters, including not only the nature of the human soul, but also how to work with the process of soul awakening—person to planet.

My intention in this introduction is simply to provide an initial framework for understanding this particular approach to working with the soul, soul awakening, soul process, and the soul journey. I deliberately present the parameters briefly here, so that you can get a general feel for the topic as a whole and I can begin to open the field of inquiry we are working in.

Note that I write about the parameters and, later, the details within them, in an intentionally informal and personal way, reporting how they formed from my experience and contributed to my understanding. There is no drive here to "prove a point," or to reject, or even compare, other perspectives that may differ from mine. To me the whole endeavor is too complex and mysterious for that. Rather, I want simply to share what I have come to understand about the soul and the process of soul awakening, and what I am learning still, in the hopes that it may be useful to others similarly engaged in this question of "who we are and who we can become." I believe the informality will be a better catalyst to both the experience and the understanding I am trying to illumine. The following, then, are the parameters of this process of soul awakening that have been most useful to me in my work and life.

Soul

I have come to use the word "soul" to express the experience of the core of consciousness in each of us that holds the potential and pattern of our full, unique, maturity. This soul is seeking realization and expression in our everyday life and its presence is within us from birth to death. I am not using the word in its religious connotation, though this connection can be made, but rather in its existential meaning of human vitality and depth, core qualities and values, essential meaning, and particular life intention/ purpose/ direction. Synonyms might be "essence," "true nature," "core being," "Self, " or "Higher Self. "From all these I have chosen to use the word "soul" because of its common parlance, its suggestion of the very heart of any matter, and its emotional and imaginative connotations which evoke direct non-rational experience and mystery. "Self" and "Higher Self, " particularly, seem too clinical and abstract to me, though they are synonymous. Perhaps it is the poet in me that prefers "soul," but it has seemed also over the years that this term is easier and more immediate to people's understanding and their experience of soul can be more readily evoked by using it.

The soul is within us, whether we are aware of it, or not. It is an essential and central aspect of our human consciousness. I see it as the core of our personhood, comparable to the nucleus of a cell. It can be conceived as spirit, or holy fire, for its core aspect is being and aliveness. It also has power, and so I sometimes use the term "soul force" to describe this experience. I think of the soul as Life seeking to live itself more deeply through us in the particular ways our life is composed. It can also be conceived, and described, as deep beauty, love, wisdom, or interrelatedness with all living beings within a living universe.

Soul is who we are at the deepest level of our being. It is a guiding and sustaining presence within our experience, and our lives can be conceived as setting out, knowingly or unknowingly, to find and nourish this source and force within us, to confront the blocks we encounter, and to work out the ways to express it.

Soul Journey

I have come to see our human life, individual and collective, as a journey of the soul on earth. This soul journey is universal and archetypal in all cultures, though named in myriad different ways. It is basically mysterious, with many vicissitudes and complexities, and emerges as the gradual maturation of the human being proceeds. It is fundamentally unique to each person in the details, and at the same time there are common themes, challenges, and principles that emerge in its different phases. It takes a long time—a full life—and even then is never fully understood, but rather remains "wild" and open and incomplete. It proceeds inexorably and does not depend on our awareness, and yet, if we do choose to become aware of it, we can better cooperate with, and support, our own soul journey.

Further, I have come to see this soul journey as an expression of a deep need, even drive, within us to seek the fulfillment of our human wholeness and to realize the destiny we sense is ours at this core level. Many obstacles, inner and outer, always appear, and the journey is never easy, and yet something in us is compelled to take it. It is a central aspect of human experience. The soul journey includes all of our experience, light and dark, high and low, and over the course of a lifetime by taking it we seek to include, integrate, and synthesize all this experience. It proceeds for the most part by a series of small steps, but there are also times of crisis and turning points where old outgrown ways are shattered, or released, and new patterns and possibilities emerge. It is never over, and yet it has a recognizable shape and trajectory that can be revealed to, and sustained by, us.

Consciousness

The perspective I hold here is that human consciousness influences, and even determines, attitude and behavior, and that there exists an inner life that shapes our outer one. Environment and heredity have their place in how we live, and need to be factored in, but I have seen again and again the power of the inner life, once awakened, to shape our outer life in ways that are most consonant with our soul and who we most truly are.

This inner life takes the form of dreams and intuitions, feelings and understandings, insights and images, gestures and sensations. It carries a richness and depth of experience that the soul can make good use of, and it greatly enriches outer life with its presence. Further, it contains patterns that are at work in the process of soul awakening, and guidance as to how the soul journey can best proceed.

Our consciousness is at the core of the soul journey, but the journey proceeds even if we do not pay conscious attention to it. We grow up the best we can, even if we are quite unconscious of how this is happening, and the soul journey in this sense does not depend on our being aware of it. Life seeks to live itself more deeply regardless. At the same time, if we pay conscious attention to the soul and the journey, and learn how to nurture and support both with our conscious awareness and intention, things generally go more easily and quickly. There is less unconscious suffering and distraction, and we experience a greater satisfaction and meaning in our lives. So conscious awareness of the nature and dynamics of our consciousness and its development is essential to this work.

Soul Loss

Even though the soul exists at the center of our life, as I say above, we can lose touch with it in our consciousness. In various ways we can fall away from it, and its energies become obscured and thwarted by patterns within the personality and psyche. We can "forget" who we are, or we can be encouraged by our culture and surroundings to become someone other than who we truly are. Sometimes the "encouragement" is the result of trauma; sometimes it is simply the forces and pressure of enculturation in a particular family and society. This loss of soul consciousness deeply affects our attitudes and behavior, and can be seen as destructive to the same degree as soul consciousness is constructive to human life.

Note that the loss is in the contact, not in the soul itself, for we are at root souls, no matter what, but this can be a source of deep suffering and can lead, if chronic, to a state of spiritual deprivation and starvation. I have often thought over the years that there is an epidemic of spiritual starvation on the planet, and that many of our problems would be solved if we were more in touch with our souls, and who we most truly are. In any case, the challenge we all face, in one form or another, is to discover this core of consciousness within us, learn its nature, restore and strengthen our connection, and work out its expression within the context of our daily lives.

Soul Wound

The cause of this soul loss is what I term the "soul wound." The root of this wound is that, usually as children, we are not seen and received as the souls we are, but rather are induced, or seduced, or coerced, to develop ways of being in the world that may work, or not, but are not truly ours. We develop what is sometimes termed a "false self," or "survival personality," and lose touch with this deeper center of our life. We survive, but at great inner cost.

This soul wound may be relatively temporary until we are able to find our way back to the core of our consciousness and learn to live from there, but it also can create a condition of chronic disconnection, as I said above, and a state of spiritual starvation that is deeply painful, though most often hidden and unknown. It can cause us to lose confidence in our souls and cease to trust the wisdom we have inside. This is a profound human pain, and one that often goes quite unrecognized. There is no greater loss than to lose yourself. Uncovering the soul wound and treating it directly is an essential aspect of working with the soul.

Soul Process

This is a very central parameter. Soul process is a natural dynamic within our consciousness that is seeking to counter and heal the soul wound and to restore a vital connection to the soul. It is always at work in us, always seeking to restore the soul to its rightful place in our experience and lives. Just as we are seeking our souls, so our soul is also always seeking us, and this is going on through this dynamic, regardless of whether we are aware of it or not.

The soul process is built into human experience. It can be blocked, or repressed, and therefore slowed, but inevitably it is at work in us constantly. Of course, we can also become aware of it and learn to cooperate with it— the thesis of this book—but it does not depend on this conscious, deliberate effort. Rather, it works inexorably, known or unknown, to bring us to be and express as fully as possible who we most are in the world.

This to me is one of the miracles of human being—that there is a force within us that is seeking our own best good, and that is active every moment of every day and night. As we shall see, it is a force that makes use of our present experience to reach us, and is as close as the nose on our face. We miss it because we are looking beyond, and when we finally realize how close at hand it is, we can find our way much more easily. Soul process is the immediate means by which soul awakening happens. We need only to learn to recognize how it is working in the moment and over time and then cooperate with this movement in our experience and lives.

Soul Awakenings

The soul journey has phases, or facets, and these are marked by four distinct "awakenings" within the soul. The first is to conscious self-awareness, the second to soul presence, the third to our calling in the given world, and the fourth to our place in the living universe. There is not a strict sequence here, and the soul process will work with each as meets the immediate needs of our soul journey, but together they compose the phases, or facets, of soul awakening. They give us a way to think about the life cycle from a spiritual perspective and to understand the many crises and turning points we experience along the way to a fuller experience of who we are. To some degree they correlate with the phases of human development within Psychology, but they go further, for they include the presence and power of the soul.

In terms of the bones of this book, chapters two through five focus predominately on the dynamics of the first and second awakenings, chapter six on those of the third, and chapter seven on those of the fourth. Having said this, however, in a necessarily linear fashion, I want to add that these phases of soul awakening are like strands of a rope. They are of each other as much as they are distinct from each other, and all four in their twining contribute to the strength and power of the connection to soul and soul life.

Again, the terms I use here for these facets are "personal self-awareness" (first awakening), "soul presence awakening" (second awakening), "soul incarnation" (third awakening), and "soul realization" (fourth awakening). These terms are drawn and expanded from Roberto Assagioli's fondness for describing his awakening from sleep. As he recounted often, awakening from sleep was the first, and awareness of his present experience, but once he was awake, he would sit up in bed and meditate, and experience a second awakening to the awareness of himself as a soul. In the last years I have built on this story by positing a third awakening that is to our recognition of our calling as a soul, and how we are to act in the given world as a soul on earth. And the fourth awakening synthesizes the first three and is an experience, as a soul, of our inextricable interconnection and inter-being with all Life and the Universe.

Soul Process Paradox

This is a key parameter, and a hard one to describe. Basically, it is that the soul is both guiding and organizing our experience of soul awakening via the soul process *and* its energies are embedded in the experience of the process itself. This means that the soul has perspective on our experience *and* it is also our actual experience, moment to moment, itself.

Another way to say this is that the soul is both transcendent and immanent, but I have found that an even better way to express this paradox is to posit that the soul is both transcendent and descendant. This means that we have the capacity to observe our experience without being drawn into it, *and* we have the capacity to live our experience fully in its truth when we are in touch with what is true for us, no matter what it is. We are both observing our experience (transcendent) *and* experiencing it (descendent) at the same time.

The stunning implication of this is that the truth of our experience, moment to moment, is the actual path of our soul journey. There is no somewhere else to go. The soul path is experiential and existential, not abstract, and all of our experience, including our deepest suffering, is included in the journey. Again, by holding this paradox the path of our soul journey becomes the path of our immediate experience, and visa versa.

Part of working with this paradox, of course, is to learn how to discern what is actually true for us at any particular moment, for we have many ways of avoiding, or buffering, this recognition, which, luckily, immediately becomes our truth at that moment. This takes practice and time, and growing self-knowledge. It is a complex matter. As we gradually learn to do this, however, we are more able to claim a fuller and fuller experience of who we are as souls right here now. We gain the capacity to experience more vividly this paradox of being guided and being present in immediate experience at the same time. It turns out that there is nowhere to go but here now.

Take a minute to pause and let this paradox sink in. It is central to the whole endeavor.

Infinite Relations

The soul is by nature deeply interrelated with all beings and creatures and thrives on community, both with other humans and with other beings with whom we share the planet and universe. In this sense, there is no separate self. At the same time, we are also each completely unique as souls. Perhaps a way of saying this is that we are distinct, but not separate, or that we are infinitely differentiated within One Life. We have, indeed, another paradox here whereby we can conceive ourselves as souls to be at the same time very much ourselves and also completely joined, and interdependent, with All Life.

The way I have often put this is, "The stunning paradox of human spiritual maturity is that as we become one with All Life, at the same time we become completely and uniquely ourselves." The soul process, soul journey, phases of awakening, and these two soul process paradoxes bring us gradually to this extraordinary realization of inherent inter-relationship and interdependence with All Life as who we most are, i.e. as souls. And from there we discover that we are living as distinct beings in a Universe that is deeply and inherently harmonious and very alive.

Beauty

This parameter is the most mysterious, and the most obvious at the same time. Perhaps a way to express this is that the outcome of soul process work and the four awakenings is an emerging deep human beauty. This is not cosmetic beauty, the beauty of appearance, though it can include this, but rather a beauty that rises from an experience of harmony, integration, and connection to oneself and soul. It is a beauty that is not apart, or isolated, but rather rises from the experience of being part of, and in relationship to, All Life.

It is a beauty that is unselfconscious, and a natural manifestation of a fully lived life.

I have often used the Ancient Greek word "Kosmos" to describe this experience of beauty, drawing on Pythagoras's notion of the beauty of the Kosmos (see chapter seven). It is a beauty of deep cosmic order and at the same time it is very ordinary and present wherever the soul shines through. We often miss it in our rushing and distraction, but it is present wherever the soul is perceived, felt, or expressed. In terms of the title of this book, this beauty is the steady burning and radiance of the holy fire within every cell of our body and being—the beauty that lies at the core of all human beings.

Holy Fire and The Process of Soul Awakening Framework

These parameters constitute the framework within which I have come to hold the human soul, our soul journey, the process of soul awakening, and soul process itself. For me they are the templates within which the soul "works" over a lifetime (soul journey) on the process of soul awakening (four awakenings) through the soul process, moment to moment, to heal, transform, develop, and ripen us human beings toward a full realization of who we most are. They are the ballpark, so to speak, and now that we are in it, in Part I and II we can talk about the principles, practices, details, and strategies of the game and, in Part III, the larger implications of this work.

Holy Fire

PART I

Principles

ONE

My Own Journey: Three Perspectives

As a way of beginning, I want first to touch on my own soul journey from three perspectives— as a seeker, as a professional, and as a poet. Then in chapters two and three, I will lay out the central principles of this approach to soul work.

As a Seeker: a Tribute to Roberto Assagioli, M.D.

In my soul journey there is one person whom I want to single out and acknowledge specifically, for his gift to me has been both completely central to my life and vitally important to my work. Roberto Assagioli, an Italian psychiatrist who lived and practiced in Florence, Italy, in the 20th century (1888-1974) first formulated the principles of Psychosynthesis. In the initial years of my training in Psychosynthesis in California, my wife, Anne, and I traveled to Italy with our two small sons to study with Assagioli, as many others were doing at that time. We spent the fall of 1972 in Florence, having sessions with him every two to three days, and reading and writing on topics he gave us. He called this process "Didactic Psychosynthesis," and it included both deep personal and spiritual work as well as developing plans for professional work in the world.

That time with "Roberto," as he was affectionately called, was seminal to both of us, and I want to portray some of what went on in my work with him. I have transcripts of our sessions, as well as the papers I wrote in response, so I can call up quite specifically what transpired. He was very hard of hearing, so we would write before-hand and deliver our thoughts and questions, and then in the session he would comment and elaborate, and we would tape record what he said. If we had another question during the session, we would write it down on a piece of paper and hand it to him. He was extraordinarily intelligent and wise in his 84 years, but more than that he exuded a mirthful joy and appreciation for life that was utterly magnetic and compelling.

As we left the first session of one-half hour apiece, Anne and I looked at each other and said, "we can go home now," for he had spoken so deeply to what was essential to us, and in us. We stayed, however, and over the next weeks with him learned much about the soul and soul process that has remained central to our lives ever since. Roberto's gift was incalculable, and the core of it was that he saw, acknowledged, and received the very essence of who each of us was—our souls, as I would say now. He encouraged us to live and work from there, and at the end he gave us his blessing. We were very lucky to have been able to spend that time with him.

The Work

I want to share a few of the things that Roberto said to me during the course of our meetings together. These had profound impact on my personal journey and they are central principles that have influenced my professional work over the last decades.

Up to now in what you have written you have written as if you were your personality, with something great above which you call the core, of which your personality is afraid. But the truth is just the other way, upside down. You are that and have a personality. You see the point? You need to realize this fundamental truth that there is nothing to be afraid of. You are that—you have a personality, many sub-personalities, these are possessions, but they are not you at all.

It has been my life-long struggle—and I am not alone in this—to realize that I am not the personality identifications I have developed to survive, cope, and express, but rather a soul who has, contains, and uses these for expression. At another point he said,

Your soul knows all about it and is only waiting for you to find out. Your true self will choose, and has already chosen, just is waiting for your personality to become aware of it.

And this,

The soul can make use of all talents, concurrently, or alternatively. The central fact is that there is no problem, only a mistake of perspective which everyone does.

And this,

You have several subpersonalities ready for service. No reason to make choices on the personality level. You will be shown by your soul how to use each and all of them, either in succession, or parallel, according to the life situations.

This was a central and radical teaching, flying in the face of all that Psychology has developed about the experience of identity, and it staggered me while at the same time bringing me relief, as I recognized the truth of what he was saying. Roberto was calling on me to make a shift in consciousness, a "revolution," as he said, and to learn to identify with my soul rather than my personality. He was encouraging me to a second awakening.

At another point he said to me,

We must learn to live as souls on earth. We are the message. What we realize we can be an example of. Be a living example.

Here he was speaking of the importance of grounding soul awareness and identity in daily experience and everyday life. He was pointing me not to the sky but to the earth as the focus of soul development and maturation. He was countering my tendency, and many others', to transcend the world rather than enter it more fully. This was a foretaste of the third awakening.

And, toward the end of our work together, he said,

All that you have experienced here, as you say, "vividly and richly" is in you. And it works in you even if you were not aware of it or didn't want it. It is a fecundation, a gestation, it goes on, on its own momentum. So, don't try to feel if it is there, or not. It is in your action, your radiation, in what you have become that it manifests itself. You see that? So, no need to worry, or to wonder, or to feel your pulse. Just go ahead.

He was speaking here to the natural process of soul awakening, or what he termed "the process of psychosynthesis" with a lower case "p." As we shall see in chapter three on "soul process," which is my term for it, this is a completely natural process in all human beings that can be counted on to work toward maturity and full aliveness, whether we are aware of it, or not.

And finally,

The great problem is to have workers who are themselves soul-realized, or at least in sympathy with soul realization. The opportunities are there, but the workers are few. So, train the workers, and the workers other workers. You have my blessing for it, and if there is something I can do from afar, I'll do it. So, both your inner tasks and outer work are very clear, so go ahead, joyously.

Here is the pragmatic guidance for my professional work in the world, and a beautiful sense of the relationship between inner and outer work and the necessity of both to realize human maturity (fourth awakening). Roberto received me and saw to the core the nature of my struggle as a soul on earth. He then guided and encouraged me in my personal work with this issue, named my outer professional work, on which I was just getting started, and at the end gave me his blessing for both.

My personal and spiritual life have followed from this meeting with Roberto Assagioli, as has my professional life, in all their changes and turnings over the years, and I can look back now and see how deeply he set me straight and on my way. I am incalculably grateful for the gift he gave me in my early years when I was a young man who was afraid both of my own power and of the world. The time with him began to change all that, and I want to acknowledge and celebrate his presence in my life then, and his spirit now, which inspires me still. You will feel his presence throughout the book and I will quote him again from time to time. He is a staunch spiritual ally to me and to many.

One more note on Roberto Assagioli: His vision for human nature and the future did not stop at the individual and the relationship to the soul. That was where he started, but he saw the same principles operating at all levels of group, community, organization, culture, and nation. He conceived the "process of psychosynthesis" working from person to planet through the maturation of human consciousness and consequent behavior toward the realization of what he termed "the Supreme Synthesis." I quote,

I make a cordial appeal to all therapists, psychologists, and educators to actively engage in the needed work of research, experimentation and application. Let us feel and obey the urge aroused by the great need of healing the serious ills which at present are affecting humanity: let us realize the contribution we can make to the creation of a new civilization characterized by a harmonious integration and cooperation, pervaded by the spirit of synthesis.

And,

From a still wider and more comprehensive point of view, universal life itself appears to us as a struggle between multiplicity and unity—a labor and an aspiration toward union. We seem to sense that— whether we conceive it as a divine Being or a cosmic energy—the Spirit, working upon and within all creation, is shaping it into order, harmony, and beauty, uniting all beings (some willing, but the majority as yet blind and rebellious) with each other through links of love, achieving—slowly and silently, but powerfully and irresistibly—the Supreme Synthesis.

This vision touched me deeply when I read it, and I have pursued it in several ways that will be clear in this book, particularly in the latter chapters. But here I want to make clear that Roberto Assagioli's perspective is planetary in scope and he is still way ahead of his time, though we can see more and more people beginning to think and work in this global and species-wide context. The working out of his gift to the world is far from over and may only be still beginning.

As a Professional: The Practice of Soul Guidance

I came to this professional work of soul guidance and what I now term "soul process work" from being a psychotherapist for many years—one who included the spiritual dimension in my work with people, but still set the personal issues first and the spiritual ones second. The common idea behind this was that as the personal work was done, the spiritual dimension would emerge, but there was little sense that the soul was there from the very beginning. Rather, it was seen more as an epiphenomenon of personal work, and, in Jung's terms, the preoccupation of the second half of life. Of course, this was an improvement on denying the existence of the soul and its influence in personal life, but as the years went by I began to experiment with shifting the figure/ground between soul and personality, and positing that the soul was present always, even if obscured by the contents of the personality and psyche. I began to hold this soul presence as the organizing principle of the lifetime and a force seeking expression through the person from birth to death. From the very beginning in my work with a client I would look for signs of the soul's presence and energies in the midst of the personal content, and for moments when it would shine through the suffering and personal concerns that were being presented and worked with. Once I had shifted this context, then I could put the soul first in my attention, look for it, and invite its presence into the work. And in the midst of the personal work I could affirm its existence and invoke its wisdom without waiting until the personality was in good enough shape.

This was a seemingly small, but very significant shift, for it brought the soul central in the person's life, even if they were initially totally out of touch with the soul force within themselves. It also affected how I saw and received the person, as well as how I worked with them, for I was holding that the power and authority was squarely in each person's experience, and my job was to help them uncover the blocks to this knowing and to begin to make choices in relationship to it. The client had the inherent power and wisdom as a soul, and I needed only to help them contact and trust it.

That became the work—to help the client become aware of the blocks and obstacles to their own soul and to work in various arenas of experience to heal, transform, remove these impediments to who they most deeply were. I began also to learn that the soul process would bring into the present moment just what was needed to work on, and I needed only to be present myself and to discern what approaches would be most helpful in this work. The touchstone was the soul, not any particular technique, or method, and all approaches could be useful, or not, depending on the needs of the soul and person at that moment.

This made the work very exciting and creative, and I began to experience my role as an ally to the soul, or a midwife, supporting the soul process and the process of soul awakening as it worked to bring soul and personality into greater harmony and alignment. The soul was the guide and authority, not I, for at the soul level the client knew just what was needed.

As we shall see in chapters four and five, the soul process work took place within many arenas of the client's experience, starting with the personality and psyche and extending to the personal will, soul will, trauma, potential, and many others. It also took place within different phases of soul awakening and crises of the life cycle, and in the arenas of dying and death and full life. Every client would need a different response at different times, so the process was completely unique to each, and there was no right way to do it. No orthodoxy, or "one technique fits all" could develop, and any technique could be useful, or not, depending on the soul's intent as expressed through the experiential soul process in the present moment. Layer after layer of suffering would emerge to be worked with and transformed, and one soul quality after another would become conscious and need to be integrated and grounded. The center and the personal will would need to be strengthened and the soul will listened for and discerned. The whole experience of identity would gradually shift and the inherent maturity of the person would begin to show its face. Questions of soul calling, or vocation, would begin to emerge along with the struggle to discern the path of the soul and its expression in daily life. And at some point the larger questions of the Universe would appear.

It was, however, not a linear progression at all. Rather, as the soul became more and more central, the client was also able to take on deeper levels of suffering and strengths, both within themselves and in the world. And over time I began to see this process of soul awakening more as a ripening, in which all the elements were coming into a fuller harmony, and a sweetening and vitalization of the person's life began to take place. Most important was that the shift of figure/ground between personality and soul (second awakening) allowed the soul to do its rightful work as the center of a life. From this the person was gradually able to heal, transform, and reorganize the other elements of life so as to more fully express the vitality and beauty of this deep being. And this would lead in time to expressing the inherent purpose for which the person was alive in the given world (third awakening) and the realization of his, or her, whole human being in a living Universe (fourth awakening).

From all this, I gradually developed a professional practice that was both able to provide short-term crisis work and long-term mentoring. The crisis work I saw as an opportunity for the soul to break through at a moment when the existing systems of living had broken down; the longer term mentoring I saw as an opportunity to accompany the client on the soul journey, helping them to discover and discern more clearly the path of their soul, to work with the blocks that came up to taking this path, and to work out the details of the soul's expression as they journeyed further on their way.

As one example of how this work can be done in a professional context, I include below the description of my current practice.

PRIVATE PRACTICE

OUR HUMAN JOURNEY: SOUL PROCESS WORK

"We must learn to live as souls on earth"
—Roberto Assagioli, M.D.

In these troubled times more and more people are asking the "big" questions of what has most meaning and value in their lives and how they can live more closely to what is most alive and precious to them. The arena of their inquiry may be personal identity, relationship, work, or spiritual calling and service. Yet, whatever the focus of concern, I have learned that the underlying need is always to find a deeper source of vitality and being, and then to work out the complexities of bringing more of this essential life into daily existence.

My private practice is designed to support those people who are seeking to live such a life in the midst of the challenges and chaos of our present culture and who want to take greater responsibility for their gifts and contributions in response to these conditions. Their intent to do this may arise as the result of a crisis, or it may quietly emerge in the course of living, but I have come to understand that this quest is always a sign that the soul is seeking fuller realization and expression. These people may be leading relatively healthy, integrated lives and still the call of the soul can arise and need wise support and guidance.

I use "soul" here to represent that core of consciousness in each of us that holds the potential of our full, unique, maturity that is seeking realization and expression in our everyday life. I am not using it in a religious context, though that connection can be made. Rather, I use it in its secular existential meaning of human depth and vitality, core qualities and values, and life purpose/direction.

I have spent over 45 years in the fields of Transpersonal/Spiritual Psychology, working as a teacher, trainer, therapist, consultant, and guide throughout the United States and in Europe and Russia. Over time, I have seen a huge growth of interest in the soul and our journey as souls on earth, and over these years I have gradually shaped my private practice to speak directly to this growing need.

The work I do is not psychotherapy, but rather individual consultation on psycho-social-spiritual issues, with emphasis on expanded awareness, autonomy, responsibility, and consequent greater self-direction and expression.

As I said earlier, Roberto Assagioli called this kind of therapeutic work "Didactic Psychosynthesis" and it is this approach that he used with me and that I have described. It involves consideration of a spectrum of spiritual, psychological, and political/social issues as they emerge in the soul process. The permutations and combinations are infinite, and as a result, the work is never boring or rote. Rather, it is always seeking to affirm and support the presence of the soul in a life and work out the details of how this vital force, this holy fire, gets expressed and grounded in ordinary living. It means taking the soul seriously at the very beginning as a central presence and force in our lives and then learning to collaborate with this force in working out the details of awakening, incarnation, and realization.

It took me years to figure out how to do this work as a guide and mentor and how to teach this way of working to other professionals.

And I am still in this process and hope I will have some more years to further develop its perspective and orientation, and to deepen my understanding and skill in working this way with others.

As a Poet: The Soul Canticles

These poems, "The Soul Canticles," express the soul journey I am exploring in this book through a poetic medium. The poems came to me as a quartet, and each depicts an aspect of a whole experience of soul. Further, the poems journey through the various persons—"I," "you," "one," and "we"—and also through the religious perspectives of Paganism, Christianity, Buddhism, and Existential Spirituality. They, thus, express both particular facets of consciousness and its expansion, and that there is no end to this process. They call upon us to open to our own soul journey and ponder it from these different perspectives as a beautiful, complex, and mysterious adventure that we share in common, even as we pursue it in very unique ways. Note, the subtitle of the first canticle is Ancient Greek for "the soul is deathless." It was the first phrase I learned when I began studying that language.

Marion Woodman once said to me, when we would meet at psychological conferences, "Tom, one day perhaps you will just write poetry, for poetry is the language of the soul." The poetry throughout this book is meant to express the experience of the soul, and hopefully it complements the other forms of thought and writing present here. Some people respond to poetry; some don't, so I leave it to you, the reader, to decide when, if, and how to read these poems as they come along. For me poetry has been, and still is, a major way of exploring and expressing soul life, but I realize this is not everyone's "cup of tea." I include these poems, on the following pages, because they have helped me know better the soul and the soul journey.

I
ἀθάνατος ἡ ψυχή

In the bare beginning
between earth and sky,
a boy on a seacoast farm,
I found God's peace.
Stonewalls bounded, hayfields blessed,
and I could disappear for days
among the oaks that flanked the ridge,
could ramble down to swamp and fern,
or climb into the candelabra arms
of the great pine tree.
I moved in music—
bird, beast, bloom, sun, moon, stars—
and green time swept me, head to feet,
shouldered me high and strode,
a grass blade in his teeth,
to any corner of the land I chose.

The seacoast, too, embraced me—
marsh, scrub, sand, and sedge—
and, slipping down my stride,
I'd climb the highest dune
to calibrate my kingdom come,
sparkling sea spread wide beyond,
redolent, piney woods behind.
There, between the salt fresh tides,
a shingled village strewn along the Point,
I stood, a king, and boxed

my boyhood compass true.
From this sandy citadel, two miles out,
the Spindle pole rose perfect
from a ledge awash with surge and hue,
and when I glimpsed this slender line against the sky,
my blood would leap and shout.
Yarn had a parrot kept a cage atop the shaft,
and squawked "keep off the rocks" to weary mariners.
I, a boy, believed, and wondered
who, then, fed the beacon bird, and was he ever lonely
in his windy perch?
And did he, one day, breach the bars and fly,
a clutch of brilliant color in the fog,
to some safe haven further south
where he now sounds a shrill alert
above the placid tropic blue?

I sailed, and, as I grew, grew bolder,
'til the Spindle marked my term.
With boat and dog I'd roam
the river ways and marsh,
then make for the harbor's mouth.
There, rounding the Point of Rocks,
sea swell lifting my bow, tide tugging board,
I'd spy that line and cage,
sheet in and hold her close
to the smoky sou'wester haze.
Behind, the coast would fall away,
the bathers tiny specks along the beach,
and I, a pilgrim on the briny deep,
weather and sail my sole salvation,

would bear straight out to sea.
Always the rounding magnificent,
the game to see how close to the growling rocks to come,
a glance if just perchance the parrot had returned,
then sheets paid out as the boat swung off the wind
and drove for home.

In such times sea, sun, sky, and earth sufficed.
How little I knew was of no account—
the firmament itself was love.

II
Wherever two, or more, are gathered

Yet somewhere in these years
the heart set out to break,
feet stepped beyond the bounds,
began the climb.
Perhaps a dream, or shadow,
sliding shy behind your eyes,
disturbed this innocence,
or yearning stirred your limbs.
Perhaps the stars stopped singing
and darkness figured shapes
that twined their arms around you,
drew you out beyond the ring of fire,
promising the world.

Somehow you knew to thread among the rocks
and pick a course through boulders
seemingly set to thwart.
Never did you guess the path
would one day swallow light,
for Lady Luck conspired
and every turn revealed a vista
redolent and new, bequeathed you
power and an upstart joy.
Only later, when dusk with its shadings
crept along the ledges, or lit on
overhanging branches to attend
your least false move,
did you suddenly recall

the unkind face at the window
and whispers low behind the wall.

The deeper you traveled, the more you tasted,
the more you could not keep from grasping,
darting here, now there—this, now that—
to sate your ravening appetite.
You grew through things and places,
peopled your life with pleasure,
drained each glass as if it were the last.
Yet slowly, imperceptible, the darkness
gathered in the corners of your eyes,
outlines dimmed that once had been so clear,
and shadow shrouded even those you loved.
At first you struggled to contain the shades,
forged on to brighter climes,
but in the end such easy manly strength
failed its muster and among these swirling agonies
you foundered, offered up your breath, became a ghost.
Now dying consecrates the world, fate confounds,
you fall through whorls of midnight without one star
and stumble, senseless, in your stammered mind.
And only when the shadows stretch the longest,
quite suddenly you burst from blank oblivion
into land you had not seen before,
though its beauty hovered constant at your side
and the course across it called your name.

Who has not known this sundering
and reach of some great hand through darkness
to lift you where you lay exhausted—by fear,
by struggle, by silent discontent?

You bow in humble gratitude before such blessing,
then press on.
dark/light, day/night,
some point within coheres
and lets you swing between the poles more easily.
Your heart revives and room to breathe appears,
your body reassembles, mind renews.
Somehow the way is clear,
though still the path leads on through rock,
and starlight rules.

III
To save all sentient beings

Just after death the room is quietest,
breath sucked in before such peace.
Right here the path turns back upon itself,
begins to narrow and descend.
One steps more gently, circumspect,
the taste of dying on the tongue.
One sits more often by the dusty road,
letting the pilgrims pass—
these folk in ragged clothes,
children hungry, old ones
stooped with loss.
One leaves the cry unanswered,
rather rests, eyes wide,
to witness all that shimmers
between earth and sky.
One measures every step with breath—
no rush to grasp the fleeting day—
but rather strolls with empty hands,
content to watch all happening rise and fall away.
One travels light,
dispensing burdens at each turn.
Older, one stanches wounds with pardon,
lets holy imperfection be.
Still, the path winds down
through cypress trees,
spreads its turnings in meander
graced by equanimity.

One's willing now to be alone upon the road—
by night the stars, by day fierce sun, or rain.
One learns to praise their progress
and to cherish emptiness as love.
One waits at crossroads, patient,
trusting no one path leads home.
With the way itself obscured,
one turns and turns again unceasing,
while the great poles roar and whisper
in the now well-tempered heart.

IV

Love Now

Strange this journey leading
in the end no where but here,
the path our breathing,
the road our blood.
Yet every step is needed to arrive
where beauty inundates our veins,
suffuses living flesh with darkened light.
No wonder we, so long the wanderers,
can't see at first we're home,
and reach among our gatherings
for further guidance and a map of God.
It seems we've garnered just the things
we needed to resume our way—
wisdom, knowledge, skill, endurance—
but no route opens—up, or down—
no inner finger points, or probes,
no voice conspires to draw us on.
And yet such sweetness now surrounds,
such nearby celebration,
we scarce can breathe—
no more from ancient fear,
but from this standing still
so close to God.
Amazed, we wonder can this be—
our bodies rooted in the firmament,
sun, moon, stars, and earth confiding
in our hearts and minds?

What is this marvel of a world
that no more falls away
and leaves us longing,
but presses close to see
its cherished progeny?
Stunned by love, we sense
the primal innocence returned,
but nearby dark still spreads its wings.
No, this is new, unknown and intricate,
something of earthy fuse and force
that pours through every living thing.
Here, yes, here is home at last!
We step across the threshold stone,
alive as we have never been,
yet somehow also knowing this was ours
at every step along the way.
And God, who once embraced,
then bade farewell, is here again
so near we breathe together one vast love.

O who can say when earth will end?
Not I, nor you, nor one,
but some sweet breath
that sweeps the planet's face
to keep us company as we lose
and find again our O so ever
human grace.

TWO

Soul Physics

I want now to set out in more detail the findings of this search on the soul and the process of soul awakening. Chapter two, "Soul Physics," takes on the nature of the soul as I have come to understand it, and chapter three, "Soul Process," reports on the dynamics of soul awakening, "soul process," as I call it, and how it works in our experience toward soul realization. Both topics are complex, and, as I have said, do not easily submit themselves to words. Over the years, however, I have found some ideas that have been of great meaning and use to me, and I want to try to express them, in the hopes that they may be useful to others with similar interests and concerns.

A request: In reading these two next chapters, try to stay as close as you can to your own experience and to the words that you might choose to express what I am describing. I have chosen to use certain words and ideas, but these are not the experience itself. In fact, what is most wonderful about the soul and soul process is that each of us finds those words and ideas that best support these experiences within us, and that is what is most important and brings life to the experience. In working with yourself, or with others, therefore, it is always important to listen for just how this experience of the soul is being described and affirm this. Otherwise, we are at the beginning of dogma and the imposition of ideas that die quickly and/or become oppressive. In this way of working with the soul, immediate and unique experience is prime. Understanding may follow, or not, but it is not primary, useful as it can be, when rightly used, to support living experience. The following, then, are some of the findings that have come to me over the years of work with myself, and many others, on the soul's journey on earth.

Nature of Soul

This took a long time to come clear for me, because for years I thought that the core of the soul was meaning and a sense of purpose in life. The moment that something else dawned on me was in watching the interview of Joseph Campbell by Bill Moyers where Bill asks, "Joe, isn't it true that all people are searching for meaning?" Joseph Campbell replies, with a twinkle in his eye, "No, Bill, people are looking for an experience of being fully alive—the rapture of being fully alive." At that moment I realized that the core of the soul is vitality and aliveness, not meaning and purpose. This was a revelation, and it helped me understand the Buddhist idea of No-self and the shamanic idea of becoming " a hollow bone." At the core of the soul there was no content, just pure aliveness and being. Eureka!

"Fully Alive"

From that deep aliveness, then, I could see in myself and in others an intent developing to express what we can call the will of the spirit, or soul, and emerging from that the intent I came to call the "pattern of spiritual maturity" (PSM). This is the blueprint, so to speak, for incarnation, a bit like the acorn having within it the blueprint of the oak it can become. And from there I could see a further differentiation of this vital soul force into energetic qualities that were part of the unfolding of the pattern of maturing expression—the four awakenings—over the course of a lifetime. These qualities would eventually take form in, and animate, the structures of the personality (subpersonalities) and be grounded in specific related attitudes and behaviors, but here they were formless qualified potential. Then came the center of consciousness, the "fair witness," "the observer," or the "I," who exists at the very center of our personal consciousness and is the seat of the personal will. This was the soul at the most personal level at the very center of our personality. All this is soul.

I also saw that there was a flow of vital force, or soul force, from a universal aliveness, or spirit, right down through these levels to the "I"—the soul at its most personal level. Figure 1 represents this as best as is possible, given the mysterious nature of the soul: Eternal Spirit-unique aliveness/being-soul intent-pattern of spiritual maturity-soul qualities-presence/"I"—universal to particular in one flow of vital force from the Eternal to the Now.

This configuration of the soul's nature, as it became clearer to me, enabled me to conceive the soul as both universal and particular at the same time, and to embrace the paradox I spoke of in the introduction. This is what Assagioli was talking to me about—that I needed to recognize this fundamental nature of the soul and learn to live the whole spectrum, from universal to particular. It took me years to figure this out, but it makes good sense to me now, for it enables us both to embrace the spectrum's paradox and also to discern just what aspect of the soul we are working with at the moment. Sometimes it is the experience of aliveness, or spirit, sometimes it is an issue of meaning and purpose, sometimes it is the Pattern of Spiritual Maturity, or a particular soul quality that needs strengthening, and sometimes it is a concrete choice that

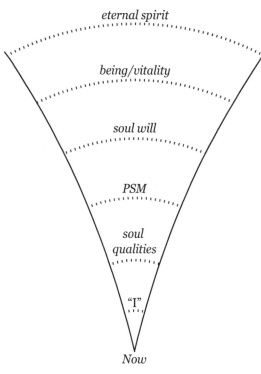

Figure 1
Nature of Soul

needs to be made by the personal will in alignment with the soul will. All this and more is soul.

I can't tell you adequately the difference that this made in my own experience and understanding of my soul and of my soul process work with others. It was as if someone had twisted a lens of a telescope and suddenly I saw the stars very clearly. It made so much sense that the core of the soul would be rooted in Universal Being and Vitality, that this was the source of the soul force and aliveness within a human being—and at the same time this state of being "fully alive" could be stepped down through the particular aspects of the human experience to the concrete attitudes and behaviors that we could choose to express in our daily lives. So amazing to realize!

I could see that through the present moment we could contact the Eternal, and, vice versa, the Eternal could be present in the Here and Now.

Take a moment to see if you can feel this spectrum within you and the flow of soul force within it.

Experiential Presence

A second way I found to conceive the nature of the soul was as experiential presence. Again the first aspect of this presence would be the eternal/universal/ being, interrelated with All Life, but it includes also this stepping down, so to speak, of the "soul force" into our particular presence. Further, I discovered that the vitality of the soul, stepped down into experiential presence, generates what I came to call a "soul force field" of energy which is quite tangible, and which will wax and wane in strength according to how deep our connection is to our soul. This is sometimes referred to as "radiance," and can also be thought of as the "holy fire" that titles this book. This soul force field, a radiation of soul presence, enhances and supports the working of the soul process in ourselves and others. The field can contain both movement and resistance in the soul process, and it works to use both to further the phases of awakening in the soul within our personal lives. The practice of experiential presence brings contact with our own soul, which then generates the soul force field, which in turn quickens the soul process within us.

Experiential presence is the touchstone of the soul. In all the years of my teaching and guiding I have found that this experience of experiential presence is the *sine qua non* of soul process work, whether directed to our own experience, or to another's with whom we are working. Note here that I use the word "experiential" to describe the experience of presence, because presence is not something you do just with your mind, or even your feelings. It is a total experience of body-feelings-mind infused with soul force. And at root it is an existential experience of Being.

Holding the Opposites

A third way I have come to describe the nature of the soul is our capacity to hold any polarity we may experience without choosing either pole, so that the soul becomes a point of synthesis, or wholeness. Assagioli used to say again and again, "Never either/or; always both/and," and he would often speak about refusing to choose on the personal level so that the intent of the soul would emerge in the synthesis. I was used to choosing between opposites and struggling with the conflict, and it took me a long time to realize that, if I held both, something quite new would emerge and I would stay connected to who I most was. From this experience I realized that the soul could be conceived as our capacity to hold all polarities in our experience, inner and outer, to embrace and accept both poles, and then let the process of synthesis, in which something entirely new emerges, work. How different this is from the polarization that so characterizes our lives now! By learning to do this I also saw that we touch the human wholeness of which we as souls are capable and which is our true nature.

These three ways, then, are means to conceive the nature and experience of soul and to give us ways to work within that experience.

In the first the experience begins in universal aliveness and is stepped down in ways that enable the soul to guide, develop, and eventually infuse the personality with its force, meaning, and purpose. In the second experiential presence opens the door to the soul and soul process and generates a soul force field. And in the third the door is kept open by holding both sides of any polarity and allowing the synthesis to emerge. We will soon see that there are many blocks to this happening, and much to be worked through to make and sustain this contact, but these three perspectives on the nature and experiencing of the soul give us some specific means to explore further, and strengthen contact with, this core of our consciousness.

Take a moment to sense your own experience of soul in the light of these three attributes.

Soul Wound

In the early '90s I was working with a Dutch colleague to found an institute in Rotterdam for treating cancer from a humanistic/ spiritual perspective. During the course of working with one client, my colleague, Marco deVries, reported to me that this client had had the experience of not being fully in her body, but of holding back, and she spoke of not trusting Life and that her soul was wounded. I pricked up my ears, and we began to explore this idea that the connection to the soul could be wounded, or attenuated, by trauma, and/or life circumstances. It was not that it was broken, but it became "lost" and the person no longer was in touch with, or trusted and had confidence in, this deep source of vitality and life force within.

How had this come about? As we explored this further with other clients, both in Holland and in the USA, it seemed that the soul wound was an experience of being "unwelcome"; that the child, in most cases, was not seen and received and loved as the soul he/she was, and this was deeply painful. We saw that the pain was quickly buffered in many different ways, some socially functional, some not—and the core of the wound was soon hidden, but the result was a loss of confidence in, and connection to, the soul.

This loss in most cases was the result of trauma, but it could also be, we found, simply from the process of enculturation/education into a social system that did not suit and resonate with the particular gifts and calling of the child. These gifts then had to be hidden away, or abandoned, and the child had to take on other means of living that were acceptable and that guaranteed survival. In the work of John Firman and Ann Gila this became what they termed the "survival personality" with the "primal wound," as they called it, buried deep in the unconscious.

In working with the soul wound over the years, both in myself and in my clients, I have found it to be a very deep and painful trauma, a wound of being more than doing, and one that shapes many choices we make in order to buffer it. Conversely, as the wound is made conscious and worked with, this work brings great relief, healing, and a fuller incarnation of the soul within our life. Often much other work has been done before this wound emerges—work that has not touched this level of suffering—so when the soul wound is recognized, there is an experience of excitement and even joy to have finally found the source of this primal sorrow.

The soul wound, on the other hand, left unattended, leads in time not only to soul loss, but to a chronic spiritual hunger and, eventually, soul starvation. We can become quite cut off chronically from this source of vitality within, and the other levels discussed above (see Figure 1), and come to exist without a compass, so to speak—without any source of meaning and purpose and connection with others and All Life. This is a deeply painful state to be in, and often leads to addiction of various sorts to attempt to buffer the profound suffering, or to sociopathic attitudes and behavior, or to suicide. Further, soul wound and loss is a condition that can affect whole cultures as well as individuals, and it leads to collective suffering of immense proportions. It could even be said of the human species presently that we are suffering from epidemic spiritual starvation and that much of what we are doing to each other and the planet is in part a result of this hidden wound. I will take this idea up in more detail in chapter six. In any case, this discovery helped me immensely to understand the vulnerability of soul life, to feel the deep sorrow that can arise from loss of soul, and to learn how to work with the soul wound directly. It reinforced the importance of including the soul within psychological experience so that this level of human suffering did not need to happen.

Soul Paradox

Here is a central idea in this way of working with the soul and it is hard to say how I came upon it. For years I thought of the soul as transcendent and somehow "above" our daily experience. There were "high" moments when we touched its energy and were infused with its force, but then we fell away again and resumed normal, somewhat soulless life. Of course, over time, personal work could be done so that we were more steadily in touch with our soul, and the process of dis-identification that Assagioli taught was a way of doing this—a very good and powerful way. His view was that as we dis-identified from the contents of our consciousness, the elements of our personality, body-feelings-mind, we would approach the soul and be more in touch with this deep being within us. In Psychosynthesis the personal "I" is essential to this process, for it gives us a place to rest that is pure consciousness after having let go of the contents of our consciousness. The Buddhist teaching of mindfulness aims at the same end, and it is a most useful one. Jung also thought that the process of what he called "individuation" led in the second half of life to an experience of the archetype of the Self, the spiritual center, and what I am calling soul. Transcendence is surely a very useful principle and practice.

At the same time, I could see that we sometimes used this concept of the soul as "higher" to rise above, and move away from, our personal experience, causing a psychic split in us, which sometimes developed into a subtle form of repression, or projection, of particularly the darker and more painful aspects of our experience. Parts of our lives were being left behind, and we were remaining dis-embodied, or developing "spiritualized" personalities.

Therefore, somewhere in the '90s I began to experiment with making the practice of experiential presence central to my work with others, and trusting that whatever content arose in present experience was the content that I needed to be present to. I would invite the client to do this also, assuming that the experience would be just what the soul needed in order to take a next step on the journey. There was no other place to go. Further, more radical, I conceived that the experience in the present moment was an aspect of the soul itself, incarnated in immediate experience. This meant that the soul was right here now in the midst of experience, rather than just above and beyond it. *It meant that the energy of the soul was "embedded" in the present experience as well as guiding the soul process, and that the experiential process at that moment actually was the soul. This is the soul paradox. Take a moment to ponder this.*

In doing this I decided to let the soul choose, as Assagioli had suggested, and I would welcome whatever came and work with it in the present moment. I stopped imposing agendas, even of the highest merit, and sought simply to fill out and let work in myself, and others, whatever came into the Here and Now. My training in Gestalt therapy gave me the tools to do this, but what I added here was the paradox of the presence of the soul both as guide and as the present experience itself.

I experimented with this approach in group work and leadership also, and found that if a group stayed with its collective present experience and shared it as it emerged, analogous to the individual work, the collective soul connection would grow stronger. In both settings I began to see that this practice of the soul paradox led to nothing being left out, or behind. This wholesale inclusion not only enriched the experience welcomed into the soul force field, but it also seemed to bring the person, or group, closer and closer to soul. It took a long time to sort this out—a decade at least—but gradually I realized that the soul was not only "above," but was also "embedded" in our experience—soul in every cell—and that holding this soul paradox enabled the soul process to work very quickly and deeply, whether it was healing that was needed, or development, or experimentation with new possibilities. The whole soul process quickened, and amazing things happened. Mystery emerged in the soul work, and vitality, and, occasionally, miracle.

The upshot of this was a profound shift in how I conceived the soul, and it changed the nature of how I worked with myself and others. Perhaps I could say I went from holding a dual to a non-dual reality, or became a spiritual existentialist—another paradox. Increasingly it seemed to me that we could work in a way that there was no split between the sacred and profane, the spiritual and the secular. Rather there was this highly differentiated experiential process of the soul guiding, working with, and being embedded in present experience all at once as it shifted moment to moment. And, if this was the case, then the way to get close to the intentions of the soul was to be as present as possible to what was happening in the present moment, and let the process proceed on its own course, without necessarily understanding at all what was going on, or trying to shape the work, even with the best intentions.

You can imagine what it took to hold seemingly chaotic experience in this context and trust that the soul was at work within it. Yet again and again I began to see that, if I could do this, and stay fully present, the seeming chaos worked itself out into a deep order I could never have imagined, or predicted. And, along with the specific content of the process at the moment, at a deeper level I began to see that the soul wound was being healed by the acceptance, by both me and the client, or group, of this content as true for them and needed at this particular time. Taking small steps helped, and having no agenda also, but the core of the practice was experiential presence, which linked me to my own soul and generated a soul force field between the two, or more, souls, which sustained and intensified the soul process. Unbelievable, really, and yet this is one of the core discoveries I can share with you now, and have confidence in, for over the years I have seen such results that I now know this works when inviting the soul into daily life.

A colleague of mine said a long time ago, "Psychosynthesis is really just two souls talking to each other." Christ said, "Wherever two or three are gathered together in my name there will I be also." Martin Buber talked about the shift from "I-It" to I-Thou" in human relationship. It seemed that the practice of experiential presence and the soul paradox was the doorway to this experience. This, then, developed into a shared "soul force field," as I came to call it, which in turn supported and quickened the soul process and the reunion of soul and person. And the soul was right there in the actual experience as well as guiding the process, so to speak, from above. This is the central wonder of the paradox, and it changed how I worked with others and myself profoundly. In the next chapter I will go into more detail about how exactly to do this.

Soul Darkness

Traditionally, the soul has been associated with light, and, indeed, light is a powerful dimension of this experience. It is the light of awakening, of consciousness and knowing, and, at root, of vitality and life force, the holy fire. But throughout the years I often saw that the light was polarized with experiences of darkness and that those darker experiences came to be excluded from spiritual life. They also were not studied and differentiated, which did not allow that aspect of human life to be included and integrated into a mature wholeness of being. With this split the healthy darkness of our experience, be it our sorrow, or despair, or loneliness and emptiness, of the unknown and mysterious, were left out, and this was a great loss for both soul and person.

Further, I gradually realized that this happened at our peril, both because it left us less than whole and split in psyche, but also because certain kinds of darkness were able to take over consciousness and separate us even further from our souls. I saw this particularly in the development of spiritual cults in the '70s, when a generation of seekers was setting out on the soul journey and was waylaid by forces that had just the opposite in mind and intent.

In thinking about this over the years I began to see levels of the experience of darkness that could be identified and worked with in quite different ways. I began to make the distinction between "holy" and "unholy" darkness, and, in my work, to welcome the first and to contain and atrophy the second.

It was interesting that a client could tell the difference between these two also, once he, or she, had a sense of both, as if the soul already knew, and was waiting for the person to find out. Particularly striking was when the unholy darkness took on the guise of the spiritual and tried to persuade the person to take its advice; or when the person confused the latter for the former, and kept trying to include and integrate it, and it never worked. So here are my thoughts.

Holy Darkness

Holy darkness is the many forms of suffering that we experience. They can include fear, sorrow, grief, despair, hopelessness, anger, jealousy, envy, hatred and many more. All are needed for our learning and growth as souls; they guide us as much as do the experiences of light, joy, happiness, peace, etc., and they contribute to our growing sense of what it means to be human and whole. Holy darkness can also include the experience of emptying, of the unknown, of vulnerability, of mystery and yearning, of dreams, visions, rituals, non-ordinary events, silence, and letting go. This is the non-rational side of the soul, the dark that, when combined with the light, makes beauty. We need this holy darkness in order to realize our own deep human beauty and to see the beauty of others and the world. This darkness is our friend and is a key element in the process of soul awakening.

Unholy Darkness

Unholy darkness has a very different quality. It has a specific focus on the soul as an antipode to the soul will, and its qualities are heartlessness, cruelty, scorn, enmity, and an energy that seeks to destroy love, beauty, and sometimes, even life itself. We all have the capacity for this kind of darkness, though one of its attributes is to make us think that we do not, but someone else does, and that other becomes the enemy. When we do discover that capacity within us, and take responsibility for it, and no longer project it, or repress it, then, in distinction to holy darkness, it is best that we do not try to welcome and include it, but rather work to contain and atrophy it.

C. S. Lewis wrote about unholy darkness in *The Screwtape Letters,* and presents there a humorous and accurate account of how it works and how to work with it. Spiritual and political cults develop when such energy becomes dominant in a person, or a group. Nazi Germany would be an example, or Stalin's Russia. Sadly, it is an all too common phenomenon, writ large or small. The point here is that it is a great help to acknowledge it as part of the human being, to distinguish it from holy darkness, and then to work with it in ways that reduce and de-energize its power.

I had a firsthand experience with this kind of darkness in the late '70s, when I was a member of a spiritual group whose purpose was to bring the soul into Psychology through training and writing. At the beginning there was great potential and a strong group of people came together to do this good work. But as the work proceeded, in the form of a training institute in San Francisco, the group dynamics became more and more conflicted, inside and outside subgroups developed, members turned against members in order to serve the leaders, families were divided, couples parted. At the same time the thinking of the group became more and more grandiose and dominating, then cruel and demeaning, and finally highly controlling and manipulative of anyone who did not completely agree with the leadership and go with the program. All personal freedom was lost, and specific members were scapegoated, often isolated from the others, quarantined for their "bad" energy, and at times expelled from the group with the accusation of being "evil." What was evil, in fact, if anything, was the group, as it became more and more isolated and virulent, both in the immediate relationships within itself, and in relations between it and other groups doing similar work. It was a living nightmare. I lost contact with almost all the people I loved and even with my own mind for a while, all in this tiny gulag experience in sunny California. This was an experience of unholy darkness.

The striking thing is that when we, as a group, started out, we were connected to each other and to our shared work, and in the early years there was a sense of joy and creative productivity among us. We were in touch with a vision for betterment of the world through Psychology and willing to work very hard to achieve it. We were quite coherent as a group, and caring of each other. But slowly, as the stress of work increased, and issues of power and responsibility were not addressed, something else began to happen which was at first very hard to see. Certain members took over the leadership at the expense of the whole group, certain members were expelled when they disagreed with certain actions, members were turned against each other in subtle and not so subtle ways, and the separation between us grew. The group also became more isolated, cut off from colleagues in the same field, and increasingly arrogant and paranoid. The unholy darkness was doing its work, and the group was becoming more and more dis-coherent, i.e. organized in life-destroying, rather than life-enhancing, ways. It was a very dangerous place to be, and turned into quite the opposite of where we had started. It was soul-destroying rather than soul-nourishing.

There were many examples of this kind of cult development at that time, and they are with us still, even at the national level. Note that the promise of such a group was initially for a better life, however that was defined, and people were attracted to that vision. But where the group ended up it was quite clear that unholy darkness had done its work.

Eventually I did extricate myself from that San Francisco group, but not before there was great suffering and loss for me, my family, and my friends. It was a tale I lived to tell. When I had recovered myself sufficiently, I began to study what had happened. In the end I learned a great deal about what can go wrong in a "spiritual" group, and how unholy darkness works—a lesson that I have used to good ends since. In retrospect, I would not wish this experience on anyone; it was horrendous. Yet I am also grateful for the experience. It taught me the "pathology of the spirit" and how "the road to hell can be paved with good intentions." We were naïve, and had no way of knowing what was happening. We are wiser now.

This same dynamic can develop in political groups, racial and ethnic groups, and, infamously, in religious groups, and we have seen many examples of this over the centuries and decades. It has given spiritual life a bad name, but in truth it has nothing to do with spiritual life, but rather with the tendencies within human beings to get separated from each other through fear, greed, and domination, and then to inflict all manner of wounds and grievous suffering on each other in the name of whatever the cause is. In the last century we saw any number of genocides that originated in this unholy darkness within us. Sadly, we will see more in the years to come. It is an aspect of our human experience that we need to keep a close eye on and learn how to deal with so it does not take over. We are learning this slowly.

In time my life did come back to me, along with my family and my profession, and eventually a sense of normalcy, and with it came a growing understanding of the place of unholy darkness in soul process work. By no accident in the years since have I had occasion to work with many cult survivors to help them "deprogram" and return to normal life. I have also helped people within cults bring them down.

Most of all, I now know that all these kinds of darkness—holy and unholy—exist in me and in everyone and that they need to be included and attended to in very particular ways. They are an innate part of the soul, soul awakening, and the emergence of a human spiritual maturity, and it is at our peril that we do not include, and work, with them.

Soul/Psyche/Personality

As I have shared, when I first saw Assagioli's "oval diagram" as a young man, I had an epiphany that it could provide the compre-hensive understanding of the human being I had been looking for. I did not yet see the details, but I had the intu-itive sense that it was real and valuable in my search. I spent the next 20 years filling out this understanding and also coming up against some of the limitations of the diagram and modifying it accordingly. But to say right at the start, this is a brilliant conception of human consciousness coming from Roberto Assagioli and Psycho-synthesis —one that has been immensely useful to me and countless others over the years. There have been disagreements over how it works and what it means, but the basic insight of three dimensions of human conscious-ness—personal, psychical, and spiritual—and their relationship to each other as one living system has helped work with the soul tremendously.

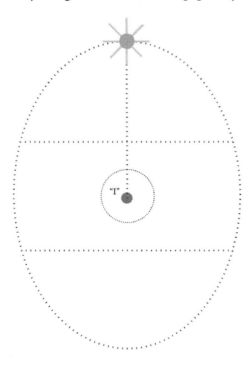

Figure 2
Traditional Oval Diagram.

Figure 2 is the diagram as I first saw it. The following Figure 3 is the diagram as I came to revise and use it. In chapter four I will go into detail about how these transformations happened.

The original diagram differentiates three levels of human consciousness—the unconscious, the superconscious, and consciousness/preconscious with the "I" at the very center. From the "I" a dotted line runs up to the "Higher Self," and the two are joined in this way. The whole diagram is surrounded by the collective unconscious. This is an image of the Higher Self as transcendent, with its outpost, so to speak, in the "I," which becomes the seat of both pure consciousness and personal will, and also the coordinator of the energies of the various levels of consciousness portrayed.

In my version (Figure 3), there are the various identifications within the realm of consciousness/preconscious that make up the personality, often called subpersonalities, or subselves. I indicate these with dots to represent particular identifications. The term I have come to use for these identifications as a whole is "personal

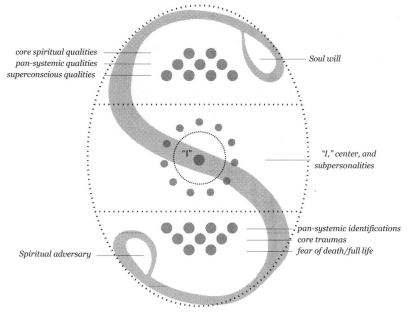

Figure 3
The Whole Human Being

identification system." These identifications have psychic roots in the unconscious, in the form of functional and/or dysfunctional patterns of energy that influence the attitudes and behaviors of the subpersonalities. In the superconscious reside energetic qualities that hold our potential, but are not yet in personal form; they need to be stepped down into the personality. Assagioli is very clear that the superconscious is distinct from the Higher Self, and, in fact, identification with the superconscious can lead to what is sometimes called "higher sidetracking" and a distraction from the soul itself.

Over the years I made several additions to this diagram. One is to portray the identification system as a circle of dots. Each could also be portrayed by a lower case "i." Another is to differentiate the unconscious into pan-systemic identifications and core traumas. A pan-systemic identification is one that influences the personal identification system as a whole—for example, depression may influence how a person is able to work, to relate to others, and to enjoy life. A third is to add the "fear of death and of full life" at the very bottom of the psyche. In the superconscious I differentiate superconscious qualities from core spiritual qualities and pan-systemic qualities and also speak about the intimate relationship between core traumas and core spiritual qualities. The biggest change, however, is in portraying the soul as embracing the whole psychic system and becoming embedded in the experience of all dimensions as well as remaining transcendent (soul process paradox). I brought the "S" down into the oval diagram as the context for all the experience rather than keeping it at the top. This allows the "I" to stay just where it is, in the very middle, and to be connected to the soul without going up the dotted line. It also allows the soul to embrace all of human experience, not just the "high" aspects, and to hold within it the spiritual, or soul, will, as well as the spiritual adversary, its antipode, and to embrace both without polarization. Figure 3 seeks to portray these changes, and they are in keeping with what I have already said about the soul and soul process. It is a non-dual vision, and existential in the sense that it sees all experience as contributing to, and being included in, soul awakening and emerging spiritual maturity.

What is missing from Figure 3 is the relationship to the Universal Spirit, or Self. Some have suggested that the star remain at the top of the diagram to portray this, but I find this too confusing. The purpose of the diagram is to show the soul as context for all our experience, and needing it all, and the "S" does that well. But I want to say here that implicit in the diagram is the relationship between the soul as portrayed and the Universal Self, Soul, or Spirit, whatever the name. This is clear in Figure 1 with the spectrum of soul consciousness from the universal to the particular, and will be again as we consider the larger dimensions of soul process work in chapters six and seven.

In chapter four I will go into more detail as to how I learned to work with this diagram and its dynamics, but for now this is both what I learned from Psychosynthesis about soul/psyche/ personality and how I had to go beyond it in certain ways. The work I did in Spiritual Psychology in the '90s and '00s was rooted in this expanded understanding that emerged over the 20 years since I first saw the diagram in 1970 and had my epiphany. How long this all takes, but how rich and interesting the search!

Personal Will/Soul Will

Another key concept that Assagioli developed within Psychosynthesis was that of the spiritual will and the personal will, and their relationship. He describes us as developing our personal wills through four stages—strong, skillful, good, and spiritual. In this he is saying that first we develop the capacity to dis-identify and rest in the "I," or center (first awakening), then we learn to use this will/intent skillfully to coordinate and heal and develop the various aspects of our personality from the perspective of the soul (second awakening). Then we make choices that are increasingly good for the whole of us (third awakening), and finally we learn to align our personal will with the will of our own soul, and let go of any personal willfulness (fourth awakening). This makes very good sense, and is very helpful to people in knowing where they are in their use of the will. I have used this conceptualization throughout my career.

Assagioli also broke down the act of will into six steps in order again to help people know where they were in the development of their will. The steps are intention, deliberation, choice, affirmation, planning, and direction of the action. I taught these over the years with good success, but here I found that I could make an addition that made clearer the root of the personal will in the "I" and, ultimately, the soul. I added three steps to the six—being, presence, and attention. Being is omnidirectional awareness, presence is focused awareness, attention is sustained, focused awareness, and this sequence leads naturally into intention that is sustained attention over time and in space. This made it explicit that the will is rooted in being, not doing, though it leads eventually to action, and that a person can always rest in being and be in touch with this first step of willing which is also the most individual aspect of the soul. Further, the relationship between the spiritual, or soul, will and personal will is clearer, and it is easier to portray the work of the personal will as alignment with the soul's will. In one of our sessions Roberto said to me,

There is no personal choice on the personal level, for personal motives. The true self will choose, and has already chosen, just is waiting for your personality to become aware of it. There is no personal choosing. What a relief! Realize this joyously! It's a relief. If you let go, you receive everything needed. If you refuse to choose on a personal level, the Self will be obliged to choose for you, and it has already done it, and it waits for you to be aware.

In saying this he is talking about the last step of shifting from the good will to the spiritual, and certainly all the work with the other steps is needed in order to do this—something I discovered over the next 40 years. But this is the essence of the soul will, as I call it, whereby the intent of the soul is fully carried out by the personality, supported by the patterns in the psyche, and with the alignment of the personal will to this deeper source of vitality, meaning, and purpose.

Soul Identity

Here is the crux of this way of working with the soul, and it took me years to get this clear as much as I have and share it here. It is very subtle, because it is an understanding of the soul that has no splits in it, and yet is infinitely differentiated into distinct experiences—in this case, of identity. I have said that I have come to think of the soul as the "nucleus of the cell" of the human being. Therefore it is completely "within" the cell, and yet has a guiding/directing function for the health of the cell as a whole. Another analogy would be the acorn containing the pattern of the full oak that it may, or may not, become, depending on conditions, but the intent and potential for full maturity is there from the beginning. The soul, then, is within the consciousness of the human being as a guiding principle and as an aspect of all the experience within that human being (soul paradox).

We begin life as souls and birth is a spiritual event for that reason. Soon, however, we begin to develop as personalities in all the complexity of that process and we tend to identify with those developments and come to think that these are who we are. Assagioli said this to me in the first session, and pointed out that I had been making a mistake in identification, "as everyone does." We think we are our personalities rather than the soul, the guiding force for our true self. We settle for less than we truly are. As I have said, this can result from trauma, education, or socialization, but in all cases, by identifying in this way, we can lose touch with our souls.

We can see the process of soul awakening, then, as leading to a basic shift in identification from personality to soul—what I call the first and second awakening—and it is important to note that it is a figure/ground shift, not an either/or one. It is a shift from one perspective to another. Both are still within our consciousness; there is no split. As we learn to identify more and more steadily with our soul, we still have a personality and all the experience we have gained through it. As our consciousness broadens and deepens, we still are a very particular person at a very particular time in history and culture. Again, my signature—

The stunning paradox of human spirituality is that as we become one with All Life, we at the same time become completely and uniquely ourselves.

This is the figure/ground shift in consciousness that most of us are involved with. Ram Dass has a humorous saying for this process—"Don't be a role, be a soul."

I have seen as well other identity shifts that I want to mention briefly, for they too are part of the nature of the soul. Think of identity as existing on a spectrum of maturity. At one end of the spectrum of consciousness are the many shifts from one identification to another within the personality and the development of new identifications as we grow and change as personalities (first awakening) with the "I" gradually growing stronger. Then comes this one from personality to soul (second awakening). Then, toward the other end of the spectrum I have seen a shift within the soul to a planetary identity—an experience of being a world being, kindred to all beings on earth, human and non-human (third awakening) and having a place and part in the world. And this is sometimes followed by another shift within the soul to an experience of cosmic identity, of kindredness with the whole living Universe (fourth awakening). Note that the experience of particular personhood remains intact, but the dimensions of identity have expanded cosmically. We are the same "person," but our consciousness is radically expanded and very different from one end of the spectrum to the other.

Note that these shifts in identity cannot be induced, forced, or imposed. Each has to arise from the natural process of soul awakening as it unfolds over time, so that we are prepared to bear the intensity of the experience and it is real rather than pretended. Pretense leads to cults and the devolution of consciousness, and the distortion and destruction of soul life. What is most important is to take the next immediate step, wherever we are, and do that well. There is no substitute for that. These, however, are the dimensions of identity that I have come to see exist within the soul and that we may touch in time. All are needed, and all contribute to bringing gradually into being a full human maturity and wholeness.

Soul Infusion

Another realization that has been a great help to me in understanding the nature of the soul and how it works is that of degrees of soul infusion; a sense of the degree to which soul force has infused the structures of our personality and psyche, so that these both are serving as clear conduits of the soul force out into the world.

A small degree of soul infusion would mean that the soul is largely blocked from expression and the structures and patterns of the personality/psyche are dominant. These personal structures/patterns may be functional, or dysfunctional, but they are impervious to the energies of the soul, except perhaps at secret moments when it breaks through—say, during a crisis, or when being moved by a powerful event.

A greater degree of soul infusion would be the intermittent infusion of soul force and consequent expression, along with moments of being blocked from them. This is perhaps the most common degree I have seen and experienced in my work and life, and most of us are struggling to increase the amount and steadiness of soul infusion and expression in our lives.

A next degree would be the experience of personal letting go and opening, which would enable our soul force to flow quite easily and steadily through the personality/psyche into the world, and this would be a reliable and steady expression so that we would not have to think about, or work, at it. Soul flow would be quite natural and would result in a soul-infused personality. Thomas Merton refers to this condition as having developed "the habits of holiness."

The last degree, rare still on the planet, would be a complete alignment of personality and soul such that we, in our whole human being, radiate and express soul force continuously. We have had a few such on earth, but not many yet. They will come in time.

Further, what I have seen, and what is really important to note, is that this process of soul infusion is not at all linear. Rather, soul infusion works the way the birth process proceeds, with an alternation of movement and contraction—movement of the expression of the soul force, and contraction that shows us where the next block to this force is. Again, both are needed in order for the soul process to proceed. Even if you have an example of a person with total, steady soul infusion, the resistance to this flow remains in the world, which keeps it grounded and focused on practical expression. As Christ said, "Feed my sheep."

Also, this makes clear the importance of personal work within a spiritual context in order to heal, develop, and mature the personality and psyche so that they can serve our soul and soul will consistently and wisely. Spiritual work that ignores the personality gets into all sorts of trouble, including coming at times, as I have mentioned already, to quite the opposite end of disconnection, soul loss, and pathology of various sorts. A healthy personality and psyche are of essential value in supporting the process of soul infusion, and soul process work needs to include all dimensions of personal experience. Luckily, if we hold the soul process paradox, we then, in doing personal work, are doing soul work at the same time; nothing is wasted and there is no hurry and no place to get to. Soul and personality become increasingly aligned and increasingly expressive within the context of a very particular life right here in the present moment, and we become increasingly alive as souls on earth.

Assagioli said to me, "We must learn to live as souls on earth," and he was talking about the process of shifting identity to soul and within our soul, and letting this expand naturally in greater and greater degrees of infusion, always channeling and expressing the spiritual force of who we are within the immediate challenges and opportunities of our given lives. We don't "go" anywhere to have this happen. Rather, we stay put and do the work and so gradually we become who we most are in a Universe that is alive and well. In this way holy fire comes to burn more brightly in each and all of us right here on earth.

Signs of Soul

How do you know when the soul is present, both in yourself and in another? What are the signs and energies that mark its presence? It is an important question, for much passes for the soul that is not, and we can be fooled. Yet, at the same time, I think that each of us "knows" at a very deep level when the soul is present. The knowing comes from a resonance with our own soul and a familiarity with its qualities, and also from what we actually experience in the presence of soul. There are four kinds of experience here that signal soul presence.

The first is of soul qualities that we all share and can recognize. Among these the most profound is gratitude, and Assagioli said often that gratitude is "the deepest human emotion." Joy is another; true power, or authenticity, another; love is another; and, finally, there is deep peace, or vital harmony. These are hallmarks of the experience of soul. They may take very different forms from personality to personality, but we can feel their presence behind the details. Over the years I have learned to keep an eye out for these soul qualities in working with people, and when they break through, to pay close attention to them and welcome them into the present moment. A person may be shy to speak of them, for they come from a very private place, and there may be wounding associated with their sharing and expression.

A second sign is silence, deep silence. Someone once told me, "silence is the sound of the soul." There are moments when we inexplicably fall silent in the face of an experience of beauty, or truth, or simply being, and we cease to seek words. They no longer seem necessary, and may even become a distraction from an experience that pervades our being. Silence also has long been a choice within the practice of meditation and prayer through which to deepen and strengthen our connection to our soul. And often silence is "called for" in the midst of conflict and strife in order to calm our minds and hearts and to restore a connection to who we most are. The silence of the soul is very alive and seems to have its own particular quality that we open to at those moments. I have been in groups over the years that were working together intensely on psycho-spiritual issues when, quite inexplicably, we would fall silent and rest there for quite some time. No one felt the need to speak; we were simply together in a soul force field that joined us as souls and our personalities grew quiet to experience this. There was no need for words or actions. We were joined at some deeper level of being.

A third sign is the presence of life-giving values. These are values that are oriented to the health and good of the whole, be it other people, or other species, or the planet as a whole. They are characterized by altruism and the lack of self-centeredness. This does not mean that personal values that are self-focused are not important—they in fact are extremely useful for the protection and growth of the personal life—but these soul values have a different feel and are often at odds with the more personal ones. It can take some discerning to sense where exactly the values are coming from, but the soul values tend to take in the larger picture and express a love and caring for Life as a whole. I love the story of the Hindu man who, during intense fighting between Hindu and Muslim sects in India, began to take Muslims into his house and protect them, at great personal risk. When he was asked why he took such action he replied, "Because it was the right thing to do." This is a value from the soul.

Beauty is the fourth kind of soul sign. Soul beauty, as I have said earlier, is not cosmetic, or superficial. It is quite unlike the kind of beauty that is so much emphasized in society and cultivated every-where around us. Rather it is an inner, radiant beauty that shines forth quietly from us, rooted in the particularity of our person, not in any general standard of beauty. At these moments we see that a child, a friend, a stranger is beautiful, just as they are, within a particular life and time, with particular experiences, including very hard as well as happy ones. We see them as the soul they are.

This may last only a moment, but it is, I believe, the deepest sign of the presence of the soul. It is so important to acknowledge, welcome, and encourage its presence. Beauty is often seen in a newborn child, before the "mask" of personality begins to develop, and childbirth is a holy time because of the presence of this beauty that also brings out our own. Look at family photos of members with a newborn. The baby's soul beauty brings out the soul beauty in an older person and it is palpable between them. And this is true between baby and mother and father; there is a radiant soul force field that unites them.

What is so striking about soul beauty is that it is completely unique to the person experiencing it. It cannot be generalized, or reproduced, or packaged as cosmetic beauty can; it is specific to the person and the moment. Literally, it is the vitality of the soul shining through the forms of the personality and radiating the deep being of our full aliveness. It is the burning of holy fire.

I am struggling to speak about this last, for it is an ineffable experience, but in all my years of work with the soul this quality of beauty is what I have come to recognize as the core of soul presence in us. That is why the first line of the book is "This book is about human beauty." Each of us has this beauty within, and can learn to touch and share it more and more steadily as our connection with our souls grows stronger. It is also the beauty that will "save the earth" in the sense that, when we are able to recognize the beauty of all creation, we will choose to live and work in ways that will restore and preserve it. We are far from this now, but it is possible, and I will have more to say about this in chapters six and seven.

Take a moment now to let this idea sink in, and feel your own deep beauty present in your body and being.

The Four Awakenings Within the Soul

As I have studied the nature and experience of the soul over the decades, an understanding has gradually emerged of the phases, or facets, of soul awakening that are inextricably interconnected and at the same time recognizable in their own right. I have mentioned these already and how they came to occur to me through a teaching of Assagioli and what he called the "second awakening" (see Introduction, p. 36). The usefulness of this differentiation is that we can sense what facet of the process of awakening we are, or a person is, working on, or is happening in their/our experience. Then we can respond accordingly, so the facet that is foremost gets the attention and support it needs. Each builds on the other, both in a progressive sequence and in a spiral and non-linear way.

Obviously, little can happen if we are not awake enough to be self-aware and have some capacity for self-observation (first awakening). With this skill in place, we can gradually shift identity to soul as the center and guiding principle of our life and make choices accordingly (second awakening). This, of course, requires further and deeper self-observation. Quite naturally, then, in the process of incarnation we consider our place and part in the world (third awakening) and expression, but, of course, we need to continue to be rooted in our soul in order to know what choices to make. As we come to express our soul will more and more fully, our consciousness naturally expands and matures to a greater realization of the inherent interconnection of all life and beings and our existence in a living Universe (fourth awakening). This realization includes and integrates the others but, in fact, has been there all the time, and often we touch it in instants when we transcend our gradually evolving consciousness and tap into the Whole of Life.

One is no better than another and all aspects are needed for a steady and reliable contact and identification with the soul, with who we most are. All are needed in order for us to come to learn to live "as souls on earth" and to realize our spiritual maturity and human wholeness. There is no way to jump to the fourth without doing the work of the others. There may be intimations of Oneness, or Eternal Life, or Enlightenment, but this is not the same as a soul-infused life. The process of soul awakening is at its best a gradual one which includes the four facets as they emerge and are needed for the soul process to proceed.

Because these are so central to work with the soul, I am repeating them here and will again in chapter five, so you can consider them from different places in your reading. As I have said, they are the bones of this book: The first chapters focus on the first two awakenings, the middle chapters focus on the third, and the last chapters on the fourth. But remember that the nonlinear weaving still exists, for the mystery of the fourth is that it is there from the very beginning, and without the first, there can be no final maturation of consciousness. Practice keeping both of these in mind—the sequence and the spiral—as you continue to read, and let them both work in you as they will. Here they are.

First Awakening: Self-Awareness

There is a quotation from Jung that says, "Those who look outside, dream; those who look inside, awaken." The "first awakening" in consciousness is to self-awareness, the capacity to be aware of your experience and observe it. This is a skill most, but not all, human beings gain early in life, and it is supported by most cultures on the planet. There are instances of the first awakening not happening, in which case you have a person who is dominated by the unconscious, but in evolutionary terms, most humans have mastered it and are able to be aware of themselves and their experience.

Second Awakening: Soul Presence

The "second awakening" is one central focus of this book—the growing awareness of ourselves as souls with personalities that are more or less expressive of who we are. I mentioned earlier that Assagioli would speak about waking up in the morning and then, before he got up, sitting in his bed and dis-identifying from his personality to affirm his life as a soul. There are many people at work on their second awakening, building on the first, and on gaining this perspective in consciousness within their daily life. It is the hallmark and aim of most spiritual practices, and generally it is the fruit of human maturity.

Third Awakening: Soul Incarnation

The "third awakening" is emerging now more and more in people's lives. As souls we are awakening to the world and our intent to be more deeply incarnated in its ways rather than to rise above it—another central focus of this book. The Bodhisattva within Buddhism is an image of this movement of the soul, as is the Christian emphasis on service. David Spangler speaks about "not being incarnated enough" and "privileging the personal." And in a bottle cap I recently found a quotation from Albert Schweitzer, "Among you who will be really happy are those who have sought and found how to serve." The direction of soul expression in this awakening is down and in, rather than up and out. Assagioli's emphasis on the will also speaks to the emergence of this third awakening in our human consciousness.

Fourth Awakening: Soul Realization

The "fourth awakening" involves the synthesis of the second and third, and the word "realization" is apt for this, for it can have two meanings—to realize who you are as a soul and to make yourself real in the world. It also includes a wider realization of who we are in the Universe and an experience of total interrelatedness and inter-being with All Life, near and far. The most mature souls have this experience, and speak about it in many ways. These are the great teachers who come again and again to teach us the way, but you can also find it in humble people from all walks of life. For most of humanity, however, this experience is still ahead. My sense is that the majority of us are at work on the second and third awakenings. There is no reason, however, why more and more people will not come to the realization I describe here, and the species as a whole will mature as a result.

Soul and God

What have I learned about the soul and God? I am not sure I can say. As I mentioned already, the shift of figure/ground between spirituality and religion has been a tremendous step enabling the emergence of the possibility of supporting and nourishing spirituality without needing to have recourse to religion. This, among other things, has enabled me and many others to use the secular language of Psychology to work with the spiritual dimension of human experience and integrate it with the psychological and physical dimensions. This has been an important shift and development in the last 50 years.

Certainly soul has been associated with God, and this connection can still be made from what I have said here, and in some cases, this may be the right thing to do. There is a choice. At the same time, and more often as not, I have found it useful to posit the existence of the soul in an existential sense as a living experience and an aspect of our human nature, whether or not God "exists." This affirms human depth and beauty and the existence of the soul and its qualities, values, and attributes in the context of daily life. We don't have to go anywhere special to be in touch with our souls; we need only to clear away and heal the obstacles to that experience and learn how to express it in our own unique ways.

This way of holding the relationship between soul and God also allows us not to split the secular from the holy, but to see that it is possible for daily life to be infused with spirit, and that we can learn to live as souls on earth right here and now. This means also that we, the human species, can mature in ways that will build up Life rather than destroying it, as is happening now. We can actually work at this, and not wait for God. Or we can say that we are the "saviors of God," as Nikos Kazantzakis does, and that God will be completed by our spiritual maturation as a species.

In my life and work I have chosen to hold this existential perspective on the Soul and God and it resonates with my experience at age 19 in the church in Florence. I could be right, or wrong, or both; it does not matter. What it has allowed me to do is to work in the way I have, and to live the way I have for all these years, and I am very grateful for that. It has allowed me to come to the understandings I am sharing here with you and has put me in touch with my own deep beauty and encouraged me to share it in a number of forms. And it has brought me to writing this book reporting my findings on the soul and soul process. I trust that you, the reader, will make what you can of these experiences, and will build for yourself from them, as is suitable to your soul and needs, a deeper realization and connection to who you most deeply and beautifully are.

Conclusion

These, then, are some of the major aspects of the nature of the human soul that I have come to recognize and affirm over the decades. They have arisen in the course of my own journey and in work with others. They are necessarily limited, for the soul is by nature and essence beyond word and understanding, and I rejoice in this. At the same time, these conceptions of "soul physics" have been of tremendous help to me and to others, and so I make bold to share them here. In the coming years I hope that more will come to be known about the soul and it will come to take its rightful place as the vital center of a human life.

THREE

Soul Process

I want to share now what I have come to understand over the years about how the soul actually "works" in our experience toward full awakening. The first hints of this came to me from Jung's description of "individuation" and Maslow's description of "Self-actualization and Self-realization." In both cases they seemed to be pointing to a natural direction that human development and maturation took, and it was a process that was "built in" within the human being.

When I began to study Psychosynthesis, I was struck by Assagioli's distinction between Psychosynthesis with an upper case "P" and psychosynthesis with a lower case "p." The first was the name he gave to the orientation he had developed to psycho-spiritual work, a school of principles and techniques, which he coined in part to distinguish it from Freud's Psychoanalysis. The second he gave to a natural tendency toward integration and wholeness that he witnessed within the psyche of the human being—an emerging synthesis of personality elements guided and eventually cohered and synthesized by the Higher Self. He, like Jung and Maslow, posited this process as completely natural and inherent within us, that it was at work all the time, and though it could be blocked and slowed, its natural tendency was toward wholeness and maturity. I had been trained in Gestalt therapy before I encountered Psychosynthesis and this idea reminded me of the present-centered process orientation I had seen in Gestalt work. There the focus was on bringing the client into the present and the truth of his, or her, experience, letting the movement and resistance coexist in the moment, and then supporting the natural resolution of this polarity into a new state of consciousness and behavior. I had seen again and again that this "new" state of consciousness was closer to the authentic self of the client, and it brought more vitality into the person's experience. People became more alive and more authentic.

Gestalt is an existential approach, so there is no spiritual dimension nor the expectation of transformation, but, in fact, what I saw happen was a gradually deepening connection to who the person authentically was. And this authenticity was expressed in the present moment and in behavior as well as consciousness.

I loved Gestalt work, and was sorry that it was not included in the Psychosynthesis training, which had at that time a more analytical orientation. There were a few people who shared my Gestalt background and who stayed closer to that process, but it was never a hallmark of Psychosynthesis training, or the work, as it was largely done. Somehow the large "P" obscured the small "p" in most people's minds.

From this Gestalt background, however, as I began to work with clients, I experimented with being present and simply receiving the client's experience and letting it work in them while I held it as a witness within the field of my own experiential soul presence. I was not confident in this approach at all, however, and almost immediately it was questioned and rejected by senior trainers in favor of the more analytical and structural one, so that I did not pursue it until later. I maintained a secret sense, however, that it contained something that was very important in working with the soul. As soon as I was free of the group, taking the cue from Carl Jung, Abraham Maslow, and Fritz Perls, I began to posit the constant existence of this natural process of psychosynthesis in my own and others' experience, and to teach the practice of presence to it as central to working with the soul. Eventually I coined the term "soul process" to describe it.

What is phenomenal about this natural soul process is that, once you look, you see that it really exists. It is not a figment of the imagination, or a theory of growth; it actually happens within us, if we let it. If we receive and accept the actual experience we are having in its unadulterated form and do not try to change it, but rather study it and learn what it has to teach us, healing and development happen, and deeper soul contact occurs. There is an inherent and built-in order, or coherence, to our experience, even if it is non-rational, even seemingly chaotic, and this order can come to be trusted and cooperated with. As Assagioli told me, "Your soul knows all about it, and is only waiting for you to find out." In other words, the soul is carrying the "pattern of spiritual maturity" while also working actively through the soul process to manifest that pattern in our daily lives.

The soul process can take place without our being aware of it, and often does, but it is far better if we choose to become aware of it and how it is working, and then focus our intentions on cooperating with it. We are freed from having to impose anything "from the outside," and rather can listen deeply to what is coming from the inside, welcome that, and work with it. An analogy would be the process of childbirth, a built-in process of a woman's body. It is ancient and omnipresent. There are things that can impede and slow it, but left to itself, in most cases it will lead to birth.

I am not saying that we just sit back and let whatever wants to happen, happen. It is not that simple, and obviously with childbirth and soul birth there is much that we do to help that happen well. We need to assess the nature of the experience emerging and observe it carefully before deciding how to respond. We need to sense when, and when not, to act. But it is vitally important to emphasize from the start that we can hold the soul process primarily as present and working on its own, so that we do not interfere with it, and can wisely support what wants to happen naturally. That is the first priority. After that, we can sense how best to cooperate with it and help it happen more smoothly. We can determine where the movement is, where the resistance, and respond accordingly. As I have trusted this orientation and worked with it over the years with more confidence, I have seen again and again how deeply this natural process is actually at work in each of us in its own way. What is crucial is to affirm the presence of the natural soul process within us, and then discern how best to cooperate, and support, it.

Soul process is the immediate means the soul uses in the process of soul awakening. It provides the steps, moment to moment, that make up the soul path of awakenings through time and space, which amounts to the total human adventure of the soul journey on earth. This is truly amazing, and even now as I write this, I feel the excitement of this discovery and am moved by the mysterious beauty of how this soul process works. It is one of the wonders of human being.

Attributes

What have I learned over the years about the attributes of this soul process?

First and foremost, the practice of experiential presence is the means to evoke, support, and stimulate the soul process, for it welcomes it, and witnesses it without interfering. Our presence also coheres a soul force field, which I describe in detail later in this chapter, and this energy field quickens the soul process and allows it to work more efficiently in the increased awareness available. Conversely, I have seen again and again, when I was distracted and less connected to my own soul, the energy of the field would wane and the process slow, if not stop completely. This is the case whether we are working with another person, or ourselves. Presence welcomes and vitalizes the flow of soul process and eventually affirms the learning that rises from the experience. Note here that I use the word "experiential" to describe the experience of presence, because presence is not something you do just with your mind, or even your feelings. It is a total experience of body-feelings-mind infused with soul force. And at root it is an existential experience of Being.

Second, the soul process thrives in the present moment, in being in the Now, where the authenticity emerges. It is the "place" into which the soul process brings whatever needs to be worked on, from whatever arena of our experience. What is happening now is where we find the soul. But the experience in the Now needs to be what is really true for us, or another, which takes some doing, for we can easily deceive ourselves. We cannot assume that everything that emerges is the truth. Luckily, however, if we can realize the deceit, then it becomes the truth of the moment, and the process quickens again. Remember all content is welcome in the Now; the question is, does it ring true? The soul process will offer true experiences of many kinds, and it is we who need to learn gradually how to discern truth, and affirm that, even if parts of us don't like it, or want to deny and repress it. The Now is the touchstone for soul process.

Third, the soul process thrives on the truth of experience, moment to moment, and as we become better at discerning what really is true for us, the soul process quickens. Note, as I have said before, the truth may well be the resistance to the movement of our soul force, and how it is blocked, but this is equally valuable, even though that truth may be uncomfortable in its reality, or strength. It may be an illusion, or a projection, or an avoidance of an actual truth, so there is a complexity to this that requires the capacity to observe carefully and discern what really is going on. The first awakening is prerequisite to working well with the soul process and its truth in the moment. Having a strong "observer" is key, and developing a differentiated sense of the full range of human experience that can come into the present moment. Truth exists, but it may be difficult to discern. There is no one kind of experience that is better, however, or more desired, than another. The key is to discern what is true in the moment. When we have that, then the soul process takes care of the rest.

Fourth, the soul process is rooted in the unknown because it is bringing the new, and so necessarily what is unfamiliar. If we want to cooperate with it, we need to get comfortable with not knowing what is going on and trusting that we will in time find out. The more we can bring this attitude of not knowing and curiosity to work with the soul process, the more it will respond and quicken. Conversely, the more we need to know, and control what is happening, the less will happen that is really needed.

It is a bit like observing a wild animal. You have no control over what the animal will do, or not, but by the quality and focus of your presence and attention and acceptance of not being in control, you can see everything that is happening. Further, because of this the wild animal will actually feel safe in your presence and reveal itself more fully. There is a wonderful story about Tom Brown, a well-known tracker, who could sit at the mouth of the den of a wolverine in the Pine Barrens of New Jersey, and within minutes this wild and fierce animal would be lolling and cuddling in Tom's arms. With the quality and intensity of his presence Tom was able to overcome the wolverine's fear of human beings.

Strangely, we are most alive and closest to our souls when we are in touch with uncertainty and the unknown. It is at those moments that the soul breaks through. We see it in times of crisis, but also at quieter moments when we let go and acknowledge that we do not know. Socrates said he was the wisest of men because he knew that he did not know. Seung Sahn, a Korean Zen Master, used to speak of developing "do no mind" (trans. "don't know mind") to be truly open to Being.

Fifth, the soul process moves through all the arenas of human experience in an unpredictable way, weaving relationships between them as suits the situation at hand and the soul work to be done. So, for example, it may start with bringing an aspect of the personality to light, then exploring its roots in the unconscious, then calling in a new quality from the superconscious for the healing and transformation of that part. It then may highlight the will to make choices, or the "I" to simply observe what has occurred and let it be. This all happens in a flow of experience, without our doing anything except witnessing and supporting it.

I once made a list of the arenas of experience that the soul process might pass through and draw on. It is as follows: personality, psyche, center, or "I," personal will, soul will, trauma, soul qualities, body, soul allies, spiritual adversary, the life cycle, the four awakenings, dynamics of crisis, dying and death, and full life. (See chapters four and five for detailed discussion of these arenas.) No doubt there are others. The point is that the soul process, guided by the organizing principle of the soul, will bring forth into the present moment whatever experience, from whatever arena, is needed for the soul journey to continue and for a person to take another step on the path of maturation. Rather than trying to control this flow, or change it, we simply receive it, learn what it has to teach us, and recognize how to best cooperate with it.

Sixth, the soul process uses polarities within its flow and works on their resolution into integration and synthesis. This can be true of any particular content that is polarized, and it is also true of the generic pattern of movement and resistance. The soul process will include both and explore how each contributes to the next step. It will not ride over resistance, nor exaggerate movement, but rather hold the two in relationship and see what comes as a result. I like to think that this is like walking. The resistance is the foot on the ground; the movement is the foot in the air. Both are needed in order to walk.

Seventh, the touchstone of the soul process is vitality. As the flow of soul process quickens, there is more vitality in our whole living system. We brighten with the truth in the present moment, even if it is painful, and touch the vitality at the very root of the soul we long for, beyond any particular content that we are working with. You could say that the holy fire of the soul is shining through the movement of the soul process and we feel it in our breath and bones. In my teaching I have often spoken of "original intensity" as a quality of a child in the early years—the vitality of the soul expressed through the young body-feelings-mind. As the personality develops this intensity is lost and goes underground. The soul process, step by step, restores the intensity and fosters its expression in daily life.

Finally, the soul process works at all levels of human organization. The focus in this book is largely on the individual level, but I have also done some work as a leader within a group context, and it is possible to conceive the process at work within an organization, a community, a nation, and the planet as a whole. The dynamics at such levels are vastly more complex, and the means to support the process very different, but in essence, at any level, we can conceive that there is a soul "in there somewhere" seeking realization, and we can work in ways that support and cooperate with the process at that particular level in the same ways.

With all these attributes of the soul process, direct experience is prime and understanding follows, or not. This takes some doing, and some letting go, but remember the experience at the moment is the soul itself in its embedded aspect, so that the experience is holy and there is no waste, nowhere to go but here and now. Everything we need is right under our noses and there is all the time in the world. Very complex, lots of unknown, but a revelation of the beauty of how life works when honored and supported by awareness and love! Soul process is a great gift that we often fail to receive and make good use of. I believe that it is at work in all people all the time, and that we can learn to trust and work with it.

Antecedents to this soul process exist in First Nation ceremony, particularly the council process, and in Women's Spirituality. It is also kindred with how Quaker Meeting works at its best. It has ancient roots in whatever occasions, religious or social, at which human beings struggled to speak the truth of their experience and receive that of others. It is not easy, but the practice is deeply healing and affirms and strengthens the soul and our soul realization and expression.

Further Thoughts

I want now to introduce some other important aspects of working with the soul process, either within ourselves or with a client. These are, for the most part, contextual aspects within which to hold the soul process itself, and at the end of the chapter I will speak about the soul force field, within which the process works, and about the beauty of the process itself. These thoughts are meant to help us better witness and appreciate this natural movement toward maturation and to learn to work with, and support, it more and more skillfully. At the same time, when all is said and done, the soul process still remains a mystery and beyond any complete comprehension. It is a miracle that we grow as souls in this way, and that we can learn to trust, and have confidence in, the process and let it work within us. It is a great gift of being human.

Levels of Experience

One thing that is important in working with the soul process as it moves through the arenas of experience is to develop our capacity to discern from which level the experience is coming. We don't do this in order to control it, but rather to know how best to hold and respond to it. A common way of distinguishing the levels of experience that I have found useful over the years is the tripartite scheme of psychological, existential, and spiritual. The experience of loneliness, for example, can come from any of these three. And it will have a different quality accordingly, and will need a different response. I use it as an example of levels of experience here.

Psychological loneliness: This is the experience of a personal identification, most often in a child who has been neglected in any of a number of ways. The loneliness is a symptom of past trauma that results in the experience of fear and disconnection, both from our own being and from those around us. The fear can take several forms, but the essence of it is: "I am not able to connect, and be connected, to others and so I cannot receive the love I need, or to give the love I need to give."

Such loneliness also can be rooted trans-generationally, passed on through the unconscious from a family system in which there is a great deal of unacknowledged isolation and disconnection. Here there is no obvious trauma, but rather a collective experience of isolation that is absorbed by the child. In both cases the child often has turned to animals and to nature for comfort and companionship, and in some cases gives up on the human world. In others, he or she develops an identification that acts as a buffer to the loneliness—for example, an extroverted "life of the party"—or buffers the loneliness with various addictive habits. But the deep need to connect to other humans safely and intimately is always there, and needs to be met through psychological healing.

Existential loneliness: This is the experience of the personality as a whole in living the basic existential fact of its difference and separateness from others and the world. In the last 20 years the importance of this experience has become more obvious. In its absence—without the experience of distinct and unique personal selfhood and will; without an honest confrontation with death and our personal responsibility for our choices; without the ability to bear the angst and dread of this state of being—we often see the phenomenon of premature transcendence into the "spiritual world" and identification with its superconscious energies as "spiritual." This generates massive confusion, both in individuals and groups. What is taken as spiritual is, in fact, simply a defense against the loneliness and despair that arises from realizing that we are, at the existential level of our experience, separate and alien beings. Spiritual cults are the social outcome of this dynamic, but it also plays a role, exemplified in much New Age thinking, in keeping individual spirituality immature, overly dependent on a Greater Being, or guru, and polarized toward so-called "positive" spiritual experience. Identification with "love and light" also can split the psyche and prevent the soul from reaching us directly and us from connecting directly with our soul. Existential loneliness is a necessary step in psycho-spiritual development. As it is accepted, as its intensity is borne, it accords dignity and integrity to the personality and its unique experience.

Spiritual loneliness: This is an experience of the soul in relation to the world, and it both contains elements of the other levels and goes beyond them. Such loneliness can arise from the soul wound of not being fully received and welcomed on earth as the being we are. It also can arise from a deep knowing of who we are and what we are here on earth to be and do, which is ours alone and no one else's. It is the loneliness of accepting our calling and destiny as distinct from all others and our responsibility to carry it out to the best of our ability. The difference from the existential level of loneliness is that at this level we experience the calling and responsibility also as part of the universal creation. Thus, in embracing it as ours alone, we join with all those who have had such an experience and struggled to express it as souls on earth. Often the connection to these souls is stronger and more intimate than the connection to those immediately surrounding us in our life, but, ultimately, as we accept this soul loneliness, we begin to experience a connection with all souls, near and far, living and dead.

Spiritual loneliness is paradoxical in the sense that we discover we are both completely alone in our life, in our birth and death, in our calling and expression, and we are not alone at all, but in the company of all sentient beings. This loneliness, therefore, is the doorway to a profound connection both to our own soul and to the world. As we live it, a yearning and intention arises for deeper connection and fuller expression of who we are, and the desire to give and receive even more of ourselves, to love more deeply, to be more truthful, to respond more fully to the joys and sorrows that surround us. Thomas Merton once wrote, "A person who has not fully embraced his, or her, utter aloneness in God has not begun to live." Clearly, Merton is pointing to the level of spiritual loneliness and affirming this condition as a foundation from which to live a mature spiritual life.

The Work

Regarding the psychological level of loneliness, I have found it useful to address directly the needs for love and companionship that the child part feels, and to engage the "I" in meeting those needs. This can include all sorts of personality work—for example, keeping the inner critic part from attacking the child for their vulnerability, or spending time with the inner child every day in imagination and listening to his or her experience—but the basic mode is, over time, to meet the child's specific needs that were unmet in early life and thus gradually to heal and integrate his or her energies and qualities into the personality.

With the existential level of loneliness I have found it useful not to do anything other than affirm the truth and intensity of this state of being, its importance on the path of development, and the need to accept it. It exists because we exist. In essence, becoming witness to the value of the experience means simply to be with ourselves, or another, without trying to change the experience in any way. As we learn to bear the existential loneliness, we can become more fully grounded as a personality and begin to find the doorway to the spiritual dimension.

With the spiritual level of loneliness I have found it useful to do two things. One is to explore the issue of faith and the unknown and to help a person expand his or her capacity to live in relation to the unknown through faith in God, or the Universe, or Life, however he or she may conceive it. This does not change the experience of loneliness, but it evokes the context and company I spoke of so that, paradoxically, we become joined through our spiritual loneliness and the Mystery to fellow souls. Usually I can find moments in each person's experience when they have touched this paradox of aloneness and connection, and through this remembering and reliving I can help strengthen their awareness of it within themselves.

The other thing is to explore with them how they can express more fully and deeply who they are spiritually in the world, and help them plan the actions they can take. Again, this does not change the experience of loneliness, but makes it creative, activates the spiritual will, and leads to fuller connection and expression and the joy that comes with that. Nothing can eradicate soul aloneness—yet it is the source of creativity, love, and joy, and leads to an experience of deep connection with all creation and the Universe.

In thinking about all this, I have played with terminology to make clearer distinctions between the three levels of loneliness. The first level I term "loneliness"; the second, "aloneness"; and the third, "souloneliness" or "alloneness," playing on the double entendre of "all," "lone," and "one."

The chart that follows portrays other examples of experiences in relationship to these three levels, similar to loneliness:

This differentiation of levels makes the soul process very complex in a most marvelous way, for it is not only drawing on, and moving through, the many arenas of our experience, but it is also at work on

PSYCHOLOGICAL	EXISTENTIAL	SPIRITUAL
depression	despair	dark night
anger	alienation	outrage
suffering	void	world pain
happiness	being	joy
contentment	acceptance	peace
fear	dread	fear of loss of expression
shame	shyness	conscience
power	authenticity	soul-force
loneliness	aloneness	soul-loneliness

the levels described above in an infinitely complex, kaleidoscopic flow of our experience that serves the awakening, incarnation, and realization of our soul over a lifetime. That this can work at all, and as well as it does, is truly moving and amazing.

Cycle of Living Experience

Another thing that is important in working with the soul process is the cycle of immediate living experience. This is a way to conceive staying close to our experience moment to moment— to live it fully. There is a cycle of immediate experience which folds back on itself again and again within the soul process in a rhythmic and cyclic way. This cycle has phases, and by staying close to these phases within the process, we come closer to our true living experience. It is an idea drawn from Gestalt Therapy and also from meditative practice, and it is a way of tracking and cooperating with the soul process.

Phase 1: The starting point is what we have called the "truth" of immediate experience, i.e. whatever is happening in the present moment in body, feelings, and mind. We train ourselves, and those we work with, to be in the present and to be aware of this experience and report how it shifts and changes moment to moment. The assumption is that truth, no matter what it is, connects the person, or ourselves, to the process by which the soul is working to transform psyche and personality so as to be able to express more fully and forcefully though them. As truth changes, the practice of presence keeps us in the Now and in touch with the process as it flows from one experience to the next. This practice with the cycle includes as well observing and experiencing distractions, and patterns of disconnection, rooted in trauma and identification—ways in which we are disconnected. Paradoxically, as we include them, their very truth connects us immediately to the soul process again. The skill is to stay close to the living experience, whatever it is, and trust that it is what is needed, even if we do not understand it, even if it is painful and uncomfortable, even if it is frightening. It is in the truth of our experience, moment to moment, that the soul resides, grows, and incarnates in our flesh, blood, and bone.

Phase 2: We often do not understand our immediate experience, nor can we control it, and it often appears to be chaotic and non-rational from the point of view of our mind and the particular set of personal identifications. The second phase of the cycle, therefore, is the experience of chaos and not knowing, of letting go of the need to understand and control and simply live the experience as it is. This takes courage and practice, for often the experience disturbs the familiar ways we know ourselves to be in the world. We need to learn to let go to the unknown and seemingly chaotic experience in order to cooperate with the soul. We need to learn to let go of what we think is happening, or should happen, to experience what is actually happening, and stay with that. This way of working helps, as does faith and practice, and in time slowly we begin to discover that, when we do this, something new and useful emerges and we experience being more connected to ourselves.

Phase 3: What emerges from the apparent chaos is an experience of a deep order and meaning, which may not make sense to some parts of us, but resonates in an essential way so that we recognize the validity of the experience, even if we at first resisted it. The chaos of the previous phase is, in fact, orderly in its own way, and it brings us more than we could ever imagine when we are able to stay with it and live into the deep order/meaning that emerges from it. A common example of this is dreams, which at first do not "make sense," but as we work with them, their deeper order and meaning is revealed. It is also true of our waking experience, when we trust and work with it.

Phase 4: From this experience of deep order, in turn, arises new understanding. Our minds now recognize and can hold the pattern and learning that have arisen from the sheer living of the experience and the bearing of the chaos until meaning emerged. We can now think and reflect on how this learning can be applied in our life. The mind is as useful here as it was an obstacle earlier in the cycle. We need to "leave our minds and come to our senses" as Fritz Perls said, in the earlier phase. In this phase of the cycle we need to examine our experience with our mind and come to understand it so that we can make choices and act on what we have learned. This is related to what I said earlier about the need for discernment and discrimination as to the nature of the experience emerging. There is a paradox here in that we need to let go and welcome the unknown of the process in order to get to the truth of what is happening and eventually to understand what it means and how to act on it. Our minds are surely needed; it is just that we don't lead with them, but rather follow the experience with them, if that can be said. We use them to try to observe and understand what the soul is pointing to through the living experience, while at the same time not obstructing the flow of experience itself. This takes some doing.

Phase 5: Now comes choice/responsibility. Based on the experience of chaos/deep order and consequent reflection/understanding we make a choice as to how to be, or what to do. We choose to respond and take responsibility for our increased understanding. Intention and the will enter the cycle, for choice and response lead to action of some sort which grounds and amplifies the learning within the context of daily life. Without choice/responsibility and action the work with sheer experience remains sterile and ungrounded. Understanding, choice/ responsibility, and action are those phases in the cycle that bring about real change at the personal level psychologically and move a person tangibly further on their path spiritually. Experience alone is not sufficient. It is requisite and essential as a ground for understanding, choice/responsibility, and action—vitally important—but the cycle moves toward completion through choice/responsibility and action. Note that responsibility is based in response, rooted in new understanding arising from experience. It is not an obligation imposed on experience, but rather an organic outcome of paying close attention to the truth of experience.

Phase 6: The last phase of the cycle is rest/presence. A certain wave of the soul process has passed and we rest, waiting for the next wave. Our choices and action have brought new experience to us; as we rest, we observe how we are now, which leads to the beginning of the next cycle, with awareness of sheer experience—what is happening in the present moment, what the soul needs for us to touch and work with in order to grow. And so we go around again and again and again: experience—chaos—deep order—understanding—choice/responsibility—action—rest/ presence—experience.

Figure 4 portrays these phases of the cycle of living experience. These cycles can be minutes, or decades, long—the time/space frame will vary according to the learning needed—but the cycles are

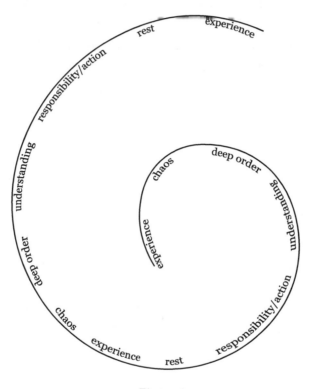

Figure 4
Cycle of Living Experience

"nested" in a way that each "small" cycle contributes to the "large" cycle. All that is needed is to stay in the present moment and work with whatever emerges, aware that at some point we will know how that experience is related to the large cycles, and to the cycle of our lifetime, and perhaps lifetimes. Assagioli was fond of saying that "A lifetime is a day in the life of the soul." At the same time, every moment has the whole Universe in it, if we live it fully.

Being and the Cycle of Experience

The context for the soul process and this "cycle of immediate experience" is Being. Being holds becoming, and it is to Being that we return again and again as the container for our experience. The soul is, at root, Being, and you could say, from this perspective, that the soul works on its becoming through the cycle I have described above, yet always remains rooted in Being. We are, in essence, Being, and, as the cycles proceed, we experience more and more this spiritual root, which connects us with all beings and the Universe while, at the same time, we grow into our distinct and unique selves. As I have said earlier, we come in time to experience both the universality of our existence and its particularity—how we are both joined with all other living beings as one and we are uniquely different from all others and uniquely ourselves. Being holds becoming as the soul process proceeds through the cycles of immediate experience, and in this way the soul increasingly finds its/our home on the planet, is embodied fully, and comes to experience, as Joseph Campbell has said, "the rapture of being fully alive" here/now on earth.

The soul process cycle of immediate experience, if we follow and live it moment to moment over time, becomes a flow of living experience within us, a stream of rich and energetic physical, emotional, and mental vitality through which we, as souls, can both learn how to be on earth and express its/our gifts more and more fully. The central paradox, and challenge, is that through living our immediate life fully we mature spiritually. There is no separate category of "spiritual life" disembodied and special and apart from normal life. As Dorothy McClean, one of the founders of Findhorn, one of the first spiritual and growth communities in Scotland, has said, "There is only ordinary life." Spiritual life is here/now in how we live with each other and on the planet. There is nowhere else to go. And so, living our experience, and being true to it, becomes a major means for connecting to ourselves, others, and the Universe in ways that support and sustain us, and all others, as souls on earth. Living experience becomes a spiritual practice that we can pursue right in the world, in our work, in our relationships, in our homes. We don't have to go somewhere special; we can practice anywhere, for the flow of experience and the cycles are always within us and our soul is always seeking to learn from experience and benefit from it to be more fully incarnated here on earth. We have all we need to practice; we simply need to know how to pay attention and how to work with the cycles in ways that lead to learning and maturation.

It is marvelous that we are constructed as human beings so that we have this spiritual resource at hand at all times and in all places. It is, in fact, going on all the time, whether we are aware of it, or not, and we do progress on our paths, even unknowingly. But with awareness, we can cooperate with the natural soul process and ripen even more fully as human beings. Staying close to the cycle of immediate experience supports this process and lays out the path before us.

Patterns of Transformation
Another thing that is important in working with the soul process are the patterns of transformation. There are three that I have discovered and learned to cooperate with, and they occur naturally within the soul process in order to transform energy into patterns that will support and conduct the soul force coherently. These patterns of transformation happen within the personality, as in the healing and development of a personal identification, and in the psyche, as in the experiencing, healing, and learning from a trauma. They can also happen within the personality as a whole, as in the experience of letting go, emptying, and opening to the soul force flow.

The first is what I have sometimes termed the "Down-Up-Down" pattern. It occurs when the soul process moves "down" into the unconscious, touches a traumatic experience and makes it conscious, so that the impacted energy is released, and then flows "up" into the superconscious.

There it resonates with a related quality and this quality flows "down" into consciousness and is eventually grounded in new behavior. An example would be when a traumatic wound to a person's faith is unearthed and opened. The energy releases, flows up and resonates with the potential quality for faith in the superconscious. The energy of faith then flows "down" into consciousness and is grounded in the personality through the development of a faithful subpersonality.

The power of this is in the relationship between the levels of the psyche. The capacity for faith is wounded so that the person becomes cynical, but as the wound is opened and the energy is released, it touches the capacity for faith that then eventually becomes part of the personal identification system. You can see this with anger transforming into power, or fear transforming into sensitivity, or hatred transforming into compassion.

A second pattern of transformation is "Death/Rebirth," in which an aspect of our experience "dies" by our outgrowing it or it becoming obsolete for our journey, and the energy within it wanes. If we are willing to experience this death, and let go of the old pattern, or way, then, after a period of emptiness, a new energy/pattern begins to emerge and take its place in our lives. We see this in the movement between life stages. An earlier stage of life in us needs to "die" in order for the next to be born. For example, the child remains within us, but is no longer dominant, and the adult is born. This happens again when the adult phase has run its course and this too "dies" and, after a period of emptiness, or transition, the next phase of older life is born. This is all held within the flow of the soul process, guided by the soul.

I have already mentioned a third pattern of transformation—the balance and synthesis of opposites, or polarities. Assagioli was very keen on this pattern and spoke of it often, using his adage, "Never either/or; always both/and." The soul process will contain and hold both poles until the transformation happens, and a skillful guide will recognize the opportunity and help the client hold both sides until this happens. I mentioned earlier that it is useful to think of the soul as our capacity to hold any polarity without choosing between them. When we do this, we touch the soul, who we most are, and over time we can learn to hold bigger and bigger polarities. So we may start with two identifications that are in conflict, or two feelings. Then we can practice with two worldviews, or two systems of thought. Then we can expand to include two cultures, or peoples. And finally we can come to be able to hold birth and death, being and nonbeing, good and evil as forces on the planet and in the species. Each brings us closer to the soul and strengthens our connection.

Toward Wholeness of Being

All these patterns of transformation in the soul process serve the fuller expression of the soul in life. They work spontaneously as movements within the process, and as we learn to cooperate with them, the soul process quickens. Obviously, what is needed in order to do this is a more and more coherent presence, either to our own experience, whatever it is, or to the experience of another person, whatever it is. There is no better or worse here, no experience to be avoided, or to be exaggerated. All of it is soul in its embedded form, working to realize the full expression of itself on earth.

We are far from this still, and how we treat each other and the earth would seem to fly directly in the face of this potential and possibility. The wounds are great, as are the enmities. The spiritual starvation is epidemic, and the soul loss, with its attendant sorrows and suffering, rampant. Yet, again and again I have seen, and I would not be writing this book if I did not know, that people can find their way to a fuller expression of who they most are—what I am calling the soul—and that there is a natural process within to help us. It is only a matter of coming to recognize it and learning cooperate with it, and more and more people, from many countries, with many languages and cultural ways, are discovering this. I love what Martin Luther King said about the moral universe. "The arc of the moral universe is long, but it bends toward justice." He was speaking in his own way about the soul process I have been describing here.

Spiral of Growth

Yet another thing that is important in working with the soul process is the spiral of growth. People, myself included, return to the same issues again and again, and, if we conceive of the line of growth as linear, then we can be discouraged and wonder if we are getting anywhere. I have come to see, however, that what is happening is that the soul process is spiraling around to reach a new perspective built from all the work on other issues, allowing us to go deeper in dealing with the issue and understand it better. Each piece we do changes the whole, so that when we come around again to an issue, we see it in a new light, and we are able to work with it in a new way. We make progress, we mature, but not in a line, and also without leaving anything behind, though our relationship to any given issue changes. The idea of the spiral of growth has been of immense relief to people I have worked with and it is how the soul process works. I am also using this dynamic of the spiral in this book to return to our learning from new perspectives.

The result of this spiral is that our consciousness expands not just in one direction, but in all directions as the soul process continues. We not only become wiser about ourselves and the world, we also become more aware of our limitations and humanity. In terms of the oval diagram (Figure 3), we can envision that the circle of consciousness expands gradually to become contiguous with the oval itself, so that we are aware of everything within that frame, we know ourselves deeply and widely. In that sense we are fully soul, which has been our capacity all along, even if we have not been able to live it fully. The "S" curving through the oval expresses this holding and knowing, and also that everything we have experienced is holy.

Transcendence and Descendence

I want to share one more understanding I have come to more

recently about how the soul process works and the direction of soul life: the principle of "descendence." This principle is complementary to the more familiar one of "transcendence," with both its strengths and limitations.

The strengths of transcendence are clear. It works to help shift identification from personal identifications, or complexes, to the "I" and then to the soul. It brings perspective in consciousness and wisdom in thought and feeling. It is the basic principle that supports the process of awakening, that synthesizes polarities, that develops a center of awareness, and that moves our consciousness toward larger and larger wholes, so that eventually we are able to experience microcosm and macrocosm as one vital entity. Such strengths are familiar to all of us.

Its limitations lie in the possibility for "premature transcendence," wherein a person steps back from an experience without first fully engaging in and accepting it. Premature transcendence can be used for dissociation, denial and disembodiment, and for rising above "disowned" experience and then rationalizing that in terms of transcending it. It can lead to general ungroundedness, disconnection, and an emphasis on consciousness expansion without concomitant behavior change.

The principle of descendence is implied in Assagioli's stages of the will, and his idea of will work, but it is not made explicit. It is the principle that underlies the process of incarnation and the soul's descent into the personality and personal life. It is the principle behind the soul's infusion of the personality with its vitality and force, and its full embodiment in everyday being and behavior. It is also the principle that works toward the experience of full aliveness and the very particular expression of our soul will, or calling, in daily life.

Obviously, both principles are needed to support the soul process and the development of psychological and spiritual maturity. I am not proposing a polarization, but rather a complementarity and synthesis that will better support the process of human development. Assagioli often said, "Psychoanalysis precedes Psychosynthesis," and perhaps we could say here, "Transcendence precedes descendence."

We need to be able to transcend in order to get perspective and to build a stronger and deeper connection to who we, in essence, are, but then we need to descend in order to make ourselves fully realized and known in the world. We need to contact the soul through transcendence and we need to ground and express who we most are through descendence. In short, full spiritual maturity is not real until the soul has come fully down to earth, so to speak, and its energies are manifest and functional in daily personal living. Who we most deeply are has to be grounded in our particular personhood, including our bodies, and in our behavior, and in the everyday world.

I believe that this explicit inclusion of the principle of descendence and its complementarity with the principle of transcendence deepens our understanding of soul process and enables us to work more effectively with it. It also enables us to respond more fully to the needs of people at this time of global crisis and to cooperate with the immense changes that are happening on the planet. It allows us to rebalance our vision of how human development proceeds and to include more emphatically the presence and energies of the soul in daily life. Consciousness alone is not enough, valuable as it is. We need to behave differently and better as human beings. For, as Martin Luther King said, "We will either learn to love each other as brothers and sisters, or we will perish as fools."

David Spangler, a colleague and friend, says it this way: We are not "incarnated enough." We may have the higher consciousness, but we are not yet fully enough in the world with it. He sees us as halfway incarnated, and needing to ground more fully our spiritual energies in everyday life. He also speaks of "privileging the personal as we have privileged the transpersonal." And particularly at this time of global crisis, I think we are being asked to "show up" more fully, "to put our soul where our living is," or, in the terms here, to be sure that personal and soul wills are fully aligned and that the energies of the soul are present in our personhood right here on earth.

In this light, I have found the following chart useful in filling out this complementarity. The items on the left are the spiritual, those on the right are the personal, and both are at work within the soul process, as discussed earlier.

SOUL PROCESS: COMPLEMENTARY DIMENSIONS

Process of Awakening	Process of Incarnation
Series of Awakenings	Series of Vitalizations
Transcendence	Descendence
Self-Realization (Universal)	Self-Realization (Unique)
Ascent	Descent
Perspective	Participation
Toward Light	Toward Darkness
Excarnation	Incarnation
Ecstatic	Instatic
Transpersonal Union	Personal Integration
Privilege the Transpersonal	Privilege the Personal
Soul-Identification	Soul-Infusion
Fully Aware	Fully Alive
Sacred Person	Sacred Planet
Heaven Beyond	Heaven Here Now
Extraordinary Life	Ordinary Life
Reorganize Forms to Know Soul	Reorganize Forms to Express Soul
Uncommon Beauty	Common Beauty

The Soul Force Field

Finally, Figure 5, which I have found useful in my teaching over the years, shows the relationship between the soul process and soul force field, generated by experiential presence.

The Soul Force seeking expression "descends" and the Resistance "rises' to meet it in the immediacy of the Soul Process. At the same time Presence "moves" to contact Experience, which is in constant flow, and this does two things: it highlights the soul process in the present moment and it generates an energetic soul force field that serves as a container for the soul process and quickens it. Soul Force—Resistance—Experience are happening all the time in the Soul Process but, with the addition of Presence, the process is quick-

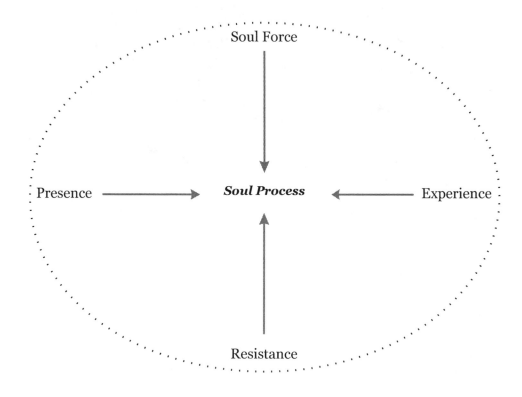

Figure 5
Soul Force Field

ened and can be supported consciously. As I have said, the coherence of the field will wax and wane according to the intensity and purity of the experiential presence.

Note again that Resistance is an honored aspect of the process. It provides a ground and also contains the next learning in the process. And, finally, note that the soul process is the centerpiece as the means by which the soul works gradually to transform and infuse our personalities and our lives.

Beauty

The outcome of this work with the soul process is beauty—a very particular kind. It is an apperception that rises from being present to, and witnessing, the deep order of the flow of experience in the present moment and within the soul force field, either within oneself, or within another. As I have said, the soul process is completely non-rational and cannot be controlled or directed from the outside, though we can stay close to it and cooperate with its movements. At the same time it is deeply and organically orderly, or coherent. It works powerfully and efficiently to heal, develop, and reorganize our personal life so that the vitality and qualities and intentions of we as souls can shine through more and more brightly. In other words, there is a unique beauty to the soul process itself and wonder at its workings. It integrates high and low, dark and light, and calls on all the arenas of our human experience. It brings the soul closer and closer to the world and enables us, in time, to live the life we most seek and to become who we most truly are. The way this happens is beautiful to see.

I have witnessed the beauty of the soul process again and again over the years, and I never tire of seeing it, for it is always completely unique to the particular person and situation, yet at the same time it is rooted in an ancient and universal human experience of soul journey and soul awakening. There is a deep aliveness to it, a grace and mystery, of which I am in awe. In the presence of such beauty

I am always moved and refreshed in some deep way, and my confidence is restored in the process of soul awakening and in Life.

Conclusion

In Part I, I have shared perspectives on my own journey and my discoveries about the physics of the soul and the dynamics of soul process. This has all come slowly over the years, rising out of my experience as a therapist, teacher, trainer, group leader, and organizational consultant, working within a psycho-spiritual context. Understandings have risen from my work as a poet and painter, and from my now wide experience with literature and art. They have also risen out of the experience of my own soul journey and the terrain I have traveled in the last 50 years. In all these cases I have deliberately shared my growing understanding in an informal way, as a kind of report from the journey, both because I think it is most accessible this way and also because its very nature is incomplete and in a state of constant development. There is nothing definitive here. Rather, these are notes taken on my journey and in my work and I hope they will be of use to other like-minded workers and travelers. We are surely on the soul journey together—a journey that is essentially mysterious and unique to each one of us—yet at the same time, because we are very much in it together, we can help each other along the way.

I close Part I with a poem, "The Journey," on the following page, which I wrote some time ago as part of a longer series of poems entitled "Santa Maria Novella" after the Florentine church in which I had my first awakening.

The Journey

Not that it is over, never say,
not that the journey,
anguish upon anguish,
through gateways of awakening, is
ever over, no, say rather
joy, sweet joy, increasingly presides.
In church, or railroad station,
midstride, mind otherwise,
there the veil lifts from human eye
and all creation shines.
Not this particular, or that, not one
fine ritual, nor fervent prayer,
but innate kindredness, cell to cell,
divine repose in flesh and bone.
The angel, now within our nature,
moves in beauty, breath, and blood,
and lifts us, even as we step
beyond the threshold stone,
enfolds our searching in her wings.
We fear not, for, behold!
We bear glad tidings to the King.

Beside the fountain pigeons strut and coo.
We sit a moment on the littered grass
among the lounging students here on holiday,
and watch the old men chew.
Time consecrates and space renews.
Beyond the park the midday streets collide
and everywhere the world spreads wide.
We, shoulders touching, arms entwined, arise
to greet our ever mortal lives.

PART II

Practice

FOUR

Soul Process Work: The Present Moment

I want now to share some practical guidelines on how to support the process of soul awakening. I have come to know that these methods help support and sustain the soul process, and at the same time leave it free to do its work. They rise from my experience, so share the strengths and limitations of that. I hope they will be useful at this most practical level for other seekers and practitioners.

A word about how to make best use of these next two chapters. They contain the "nuts and bolts" of this work, as well as the possibility of having some direct representative experience with different aspects of the soul process. These take the form of basic guidelines and presentation of the various arenas of experience that the soul process will move through and work in. The chapters also include specific exercises that you can do to gain a direct taste of the different arenas of experience.

You may want to read the whole Part II through and do all the exercises. You may want to read the presentations and skip the exercises. You may want to do some of both selectively. You may want to study the diagrams closely, or not. In short, there is a lot in each chapter and I want to encourage you to explore the material in a way that works best for you.

You will see that these chapters take the major principles I presented in chapters two and three deeper and into much more detail, for their purpose is to help ground this approach to soul work and give it a pragmatic foundation in understanding and practice. I trust that it will not dispel the mystery of this way of working with the soul, but I hope it will make clear how to proceed enough so that you can keep experimenting and learning on your own when you have finished reading the book.

The challenge in all this is to hold the bird in the hand so you can observe it and learn to love it as it remains free, and at the same time not to hold on to it too tightly so it dies. Hold these chapters lightly in your mind and heart and see what happens in your learning about the soul, soul process, and soul awakening.

Three Basic Guidelines

First, trust Life and its capacity to "live itself more deeply." Remember that the soul process is natural and built in, and always at work. It does not just happen in a session, or one conversation. Breakthroughs and fuller understanding may come at the most unusual moments, or through dreams, or conversations with friends, or when alone in the woods. Keep an eye out for those moments, trust them and explore them, and see where they go. I believe the soul is present 24/7, whether we are aware of that, or not, and is both guiding and embedded in everyday experience. It is a great relief, actually, to hold our experience in this way, for we realize that we are not in charge, and a bigger life principle is at work. We can relax and rest in this fact, and pay close attention to what is unfolding without thinking we need to make anything happen.

Resting thus, we can pay conscious attention to the process and begin to choose ways to support it. There are methods and techniques we can use, and certainly, as I have said, our experiential presence greatly enhances and quickens the flow of experience and the process. I would not be writing this book if I did not think there were things that we can do consciously that will enable the soul journey to proceed more smoothly. The advantage, however, of holding the trusting orientation is that we can always go back to zero, so to speak, and to the touchstone of the present moment and the flow of experience. We can always simply ask ourselves, or another, "What are you experiencing now?" and be there with that. We can return to this starting point again and again, for it is where the soul process is happening, even if we do not understand it, and the return grounds us and allows a next step to emerge. So, let Life live itself and then see what you can do consciously to help this happen more smoothly.

Second, remember to keep experience prime over understanding, and to let the understanding emerge from the experience in its own time. Maintain a healthy respect for the unknown, or, as Assagioli said to me, "Leave a little room for the Mystery." This is a non-rational process, and working with it cannot be done from the mind alone. It is a bit like learning to surf. We need to get in the water, get up on the board, and gain our balance gradually and learn the subtler moves that keep us in tune with the wave. We can study surfing and read about it, and watch others, but in the end we need to have the direct experience and learn from that, usually by falling off the board again and again until we get the hang of it.

Soul process work is the same; we learn from experience and with our energy body and soul field more than with our mind. Any technique from any school of psychology can be used to support the soul process, and likewise any technique from any school can impede it. There is no dogma here, only a response in the present moment, using all the skill we have, to how the soul process is working at that moment. If we are fully present, we will realize what to do, or not do. If we are trying to figure it out, or trying to do the "right" thing, or are identified with a particular technique, or approach, we are likely to miss the wave. The touchstone is the aliveness of the process in the present moment and its movement as it swings through the arenas of experience and weaves the next step for the soul on earth. "Experience is prime over understanding."

Third, remember that every experience has its place. None is better, or worse. Rather there is a complex flow of experience, rising from the various arenas and guided by the soul, that constitutes the soul process. Nothing is excluded, from the most esoteric to the most mundane. What is important is the truth of any experience in the moment, and its connection to the authenticity of soul that we are seeking. And remember that this includes experiences that are less than fully true, but which can become part of the truth of the process. Distraction and denial are as much a part of the flow of experience as breakthrough and insight; what is important is that they are included, observed, and learned from.

The Framework of the Oval Diagram

Throughout these two chapters I use and develop what is termed the "Oval Diagram," or affectionately, the "Egg Diagram" that Roberto Assagioli first introduced in his work in Psychosynthesis. We saw the original in Figure 2 and my final developments in Figure 3 in chapter two. Now I will provide the "bridge" between these two figures in a series of versions of the diagram that illustrate the particular arena I am presenting. The diagram will "grow" in complexity from its original version to my latest one, and hopefully will be a way to portray the different arenas within the larger context of a unified experience of human consciousness. Assagioli's original version is brilliant, and it was that image, you may remember, that I first saw at age 30 and recognized as what I had been looking for. Although I have made changes that I think reflect greater accuracy and complexity in how the soul process works within this container, I want to say that without that original diagram I would not have been able to explore as I have and now be writing this book.

The Arenas of Experience

I want to return to the arenas of experience now and go into them in more detail by way of description, examples, and a representative exercise that can be done to get a taste of that arena. I will go through them one by one, starting with the soul itself, but keep in mind while I do this that these are all constantly intermingling and are part of one whole experience, the flow of a human life. Teasing them apart is only to see them more clearly as they work as aspects of the soul process. There are eleven in this chapter and five in the next.

A metaphor I have found useful in my teaching to portray how the arenas relate within the soul process is to conceive the soul as having a light wand that it uses to illumine and bring into present consciousness those experiences needed to proceed on the soul journey. The point of light moves, sometimes quite quickly, from arena to arena; thus cooperating with the soul process can be seen as following the lead of this light and welcoming and working with whatever it shines on. It may move from arena to arena and it may also return to arenas it has previously touched. This is in no way a linear process.

This means, as I have said, that our existential presence is the single most important way to support soul process work. It also means that any technique, from any school of thought, can be useful at any particular moment in this flow. A Psychoanalytic technique, rightly used, can be fine, or a Behavioral one; Imagery techniques can be very useful, as can analytic discussion, body work as well as meditation techniques. The emphasis is on the soul process itself, not on any particular approach, and each of us will use what we have available. I have a Psychoanalytically trained Freudian colleague who, after listening to me teach about soul process, said, "Tom, I am working in a very similar way, but in a different language and approach." The power of this work is in its acceptance of the flow of experience as it comes, following the light of the soul, and discerning as fully as possible the truth in the moment, working with it, and thus ever so slowly restoring the soul to its rightful place in a human life.

This also means that all the other kinds of psychological work can go on with good effect, given the qualities and qualifications of the practitioner, and there may be simply moments when the soul process is the focus. When I am teaching this work to others, I say "try it in small doses, just a minute or so of simply being present to the flow of experience and supporting this, and see what happens."

If it is going on all the time, then we are not required to be aware of it, or make use of it. We can, if we want, and to the degree that we want to. Life continues to seek "to live itself more deeply" whether we do, or not. "What a relief!" Assagioli would say. We are free to do whatever we think best, and that is the best that we can do in helping ourselves and others. There is no dogma here, or orthodoxy, only an experiment and an adventure to see how we can best contact, support, nourish, and express the soul in everyday life. In this we can use whatever works. The challenge is to recognize what really does.

I have found that there are certain major arenas of experience the soul process will move through and make use of again and again. I have numbered them to make the arenas distinct, but remember they are all dimensions of one living experience. The list is not exhaustive, I am sure, but in my experience as a seeker and as a therapist/ guide over the years, these are the ones that arise repeatedly as the soul seeks deeper and fuller expression. Remember they are not "not-soul," and that there is only one living organism at work here, but they are arenas of experience that our soul needs in order to fully incarnate and express itself.

My intention is to give you sufficient detail about these arenas so that you can recognize them in your own experience, or use them to expand your expertise in practice. I will also, from time to time, cite my own experience as a case example, and recount stories that illustrate what I am saying. I offer you this "knowing" in the spirit of your being able to make use of it in your own life and work with others, as seems best to you, and as a way for me to share my own soul journey. Here then are the arenas. The ones in this chapter are those that arise in the present moment of soul process and the ones in the next are those that influence this flow of living experience over the course of a lifetime. Subtitles of the chapters are, accordingly, "The Present Moment" (chapter four) and "The Life Time" (chapter five).

Arena 1: Soul Presence
Ironically, this is the most central and at the same time the most

generally neglected arena because, as I have said, the soul is not widely recognized as a central aspect of our human development. Until recently it had been largely left to the theologians and clergy, and even now its energies and gifts are not fully utilized in psychological healing and development. That is why I start here, and clearly this whole book is written in the spirit of righting this omission.

Work with the soul itself might take the following form: the recognition and welcome of its presence at a breakthrough moment, when its vitality is obvious in our, or another person's, experience. This might be an experience of sheer vitality, of holy fire, as an energetic flow through body, feelings, and mind. It might also come in the form of a wise insight that takes the whole of a life into account. It might be a clear sense of life purpose and the qualities that need to be developed in order to pursue it. It might be an opening in awareness to the larger context of life and an experience of deep interrelatedness between oneself and others—the realization of one's place in the human and non-human community. It might be an experience of joy, or gratitude.

These experiences are often kept private, out of shame, or of being thought crazy, and, even if they are shared, they are often passed over in favor of more overtly psychological issues that occupy the foreground. So the challenge here is to keep an eye out for this arena of experience coming into the soul process, and then to welcome and work with it as legitimate and seminal.

Soul experiences are for the most part spontaneous and mysterious, but it is also possible to deliberately cultivate access to this arena and not just wait for the soul to show up. There are many spiritual practices in a number of traditions that do this. Buddhist Mindfulness meditation is one, though here the soul is not made explicit, and within the Christian tradition Centering Prayer has been popular in recent years. The exercise I include here is from Spiritual Psychology and works to cultivate and strengthen an experience of soul presence, to oneself, to others, and to the world.

In this exercise we are practicing resting at the center of awareness and observing and acting from there rather than from a part of
ourselves. Traditionally, following the breath has been the means
of cultivating the center of awareness, but there are countless ways
people have found to become centered and fully present to whatever
they are thinking, feeling, and doing, or to whomever they are with.
As we cultivate soul presence, the center of awareness grows stronger
and steadier, and it serves as a point of contact and connection with
the soul. In fact, we can say that this point of presence is the soul
at its most immediate, and learning to rest there, no matter what is
happening, allows us to experience the soul's being and vitality and
to contact and express our soul qualities that are differentiations of
that core. It is also that point of consciousness that enables us to experience the full aliveness that Joseph Campbell spoke of, "the rapture
of being fully alive"—and to sense what purposes and directions flow
from this vitality. With this practice of presence over time we become
more and more steadily present as a soul in our daily life—thus the
term "soul presence" for this arena of work—and in the world. We
still have a personality, but it is no longer the end; rather it is the
means of expressing who we most truly are.

SOUL PRESENCE EXERCISE

Part I - Inside Human World
Sit in a comfortable, alert position and close your eyes.

Focus your attention on your breathing and begin to
follow its movement without changing it in any way.

Become aware, in this movement, of the natural rhythm
of your breathing and begin to let yourself rest in that
rhythm of inhalation and exhalation. Let this rhythm
gradually become a place of rest for you, where you can
let go of any preoccupations and simply remain with the
movement of your breath in and out of your body.

If thoughts, feelings, or sensations arise in your experience, acknowledge them, but then return your attention to your breathing, so that you remain in the center as they come and go.

Part II - Outside Human World

Do the same practice as described above, but now keep your eyes open so you maintain contact with the outside world as you continue to rest in your center of awareness.

As you become aware of particular objects, people, and/or events, acknowledge them silently with your eyes, but keep your attention on the rhythm of your breathing and remain in your center.

Practice staying rooted in that center while you are in contact with people in the outside world and are observing the many changes that happen moment to moment there. If you need to return to the inner focus to strengthen the center, do so, and then come out again and notice how you perceive and experience the human world around you.

Now, add words to your contact with the human world and see if you can stay connected to your center and be present while talking and interacting in a normal way.

Be aware of, and study, the ways in which you do become distracted and lose touch with your center. Make note of these so you can anticipate them in the future.

Part III - Outside Natural World

Do the same practice as described above, again keeping your eyes open so that you maintain contact with both inside and outside worlds simultaneously as you continue to rest in your center of consciousness.

Focus your awareness on the natural world—plants, animals, landscape, weather, sun, moon, stars, earth, and how all these combine moment to moment in infinite movement and interplay. Be aware of how these diverse elements surround and infuse our lives and how we are a part of this great and complex reality. Continue to rest in the rhythm of your breathing and remain in your center.

Become aware of the processes of birth and death that underlie these natural elements and our own lives and which bring movement and change moment to moment and over time. Gently embrace birth and death within the rhythm of your breathing and let your presence expand to include these natural principles as well as the natural world.

Continue to practice presence in this way, being aware of what you experience and also of what distracts you. Welcome these distractions into your presence, so that your awareness expands to include them while you return to your breathing and your center.

Practice presence to whatever is in your experience in these three dimensions and be aware of them as one reality in which you are part and participant. Both rest in your center and practice welcoming the moment-to-moment changes in your experience in all these dimensions. Enjoy the flow of Life within and around you.

If we practice soul presence at first for short periods of time, we learn gradually what it feels like in our particular experience. As our center becomes stronger, we will find that we can sustain our presence for longer periods of time and in more difficult situations. Eventually it becomes a capacity and habit that contributes to our health, effectiveness, enjoyment, and peace of mind.

The practice itself is deceptively simple. The problem is sustaining it over time, for we are immediately distracted from this center by the many sensations, feelings, and thoughts that make up our inner personal experience and by the many events that make up the world around us. As we begin to practice, we discover that, actually, we are seldom fully present, but rather are distracted in any number of ways. Yet, paradoxically, if we welcome these very distractions as they arise as part of the practice, our presence will grow stronger. The difficulty is in the execution, not in the idea of presence. If we are willing to practice, in time we begin to be more deeply and steadily connected to the source of Life within us, and also to others, and to the natural world in which we live and which we share with all living beings.

Arena 2: Personality

The personality needs to be healed, re-organized, and developed so that it becomes capable and efficient at expressing the soul force that is seeking to flow through it. "Personality" is derived from the Latin "persona," literally, "to sound through," and we can think of the personality within this context as being a less, or more, coherent conduit for the energies of the soul, which include, as I said earlier, not only the experience of universal connection, but also life intention, core qualities, central meanings and values, and an experience of authenticity and uniqueness.

Almost all of us have personalities that are working to some degree at cross-purposes to our souls, with an occasional breakthrough of soul force, but for the most part at odds, for various reasons, with whom we most are. Soul loss is rampant, and we live in a culture that largely promotes the personality at the expense of the soul. At the same time the search is on in many people to reorder our priorities and to set the soul first. Then we can explore how we can change ourselves and our lives so that there is a better fit, so to speak, and an easier and more coherent expression of who we are as soul "sounding" through our personalities.

The soul process will come again and again to this arena to point out what needs work, and what the next steps are. This is not done in a day, or a year. The personality is multi-layered and complex in structure, and old habits are slow to let go. Over time, however, changes can be made, with the result of a much greater alignment between soul and personality, i.e. within ourselves, and steadier soul infusion.

Systems of Identification

Our personalities are configured into subsystems of identifications that have served us more or less well in the business of survival, coping, and expression. Some of these identifications are formed in early childhood, some in adolescence, and some later in life. We are quite conscious of some, which we use on a daily basis, and less conscious of others, which exist in the shadows and only emerge occasionally. Some are a product of our enculturation and education, some of unique experience and the interplay between who we are as souls and the environments we find ourselves in. Identifications can also spring from trauma as a means to cope with that suffering, and they can spring from soul qualities that we are seeking to manifest again and again. In every human personality there is a system of these identifications that works to some degree, but which also can break down and be inadequate to fully express our soul.

This arena of soul process work focuses on the configuration of this personal system of identifications and asks to what degree it is effective in holding and expressing the soul force of who we are. To do the work we first study the system and get to know its components and their relationship to each other. How well is it working, and where are the difficulties and blocks? To what degree is it helping us to survive and thrive and, further, to express our true selves? Then we begin the long work of healing, developing, and reorganizing the personality with its system of identifications so that it gradually conveys more soul force with less resistance and becomes more consonant with our soul's being, qualities, and purposes. In time our personality thus becomes aligned with the soul and there is a "fit" that enables us to be and express consistently and creatively who we most are in the world.

Personality Structure

The structure of the identification systems of the personality has several layers. The first and most obvious is the level of subpersonalities, or parts, which tend to manifest as inner characters—the frightened child, the critic, the cynic, the heroine—and can be worked with from the point of presence, or the observer. Basically, the job is to bring those parts of ourselves into balance and harmony with each other, so that they work better together as a whole. We do this by first recognizing them, then accepting, then coordinating, and finally integrating them.

In order to do this, usually we need to go to a deeper level of the personality and work there also. This is the level of "pan-systemic identifications"—components of the system that are often unconscious and which are affecting the surface system without our knowing it. This deeper identification can be with the body, feelings, or mind in a way that biases inclusion of all three equally. It can be with a core trauma. It can be with an enculturation pattern, or a world view, that we have absorbed without knowing it in our development. Such pan-systemic identifications are more powerful and pervasive than the subpersonalities, for they influence the surface system as a whole, or at least major aspects of it. But we work with them in the same way—becoming aware of them, accepting them, and then exploring how their influence can be best used consciously in the overall integration of the personality around the vitality and intents of the soul. An example of a pan-systemic identification would be a pervasive depression that affects work, pleasure, and relationships.

At the deepest level of the personality lies identification with the fear of death—one we share as a species—and which influences not only our attitudes and behavior, but also our development and choices over time. This identification does not emerge at first, but as we heal and transform the personality at deeper and deeper levels into a more coherent instrument for our soul force, the fear will come to the surface to be dealt with. Of course, Life itself confronts us with this fear as we grow older. Indeed, it is the purpose of the personality to stay alive and its solutions to the conditions it has confronted, even if sometimes conflicted and distorted, are the best possible solution to this challenge. The bottom line is to keep us alive and so the fear of death is, at its root, a motive for that task.

At the same time this fear of death limits us in expression and keeps us from the experience of the soul beyond birth and death, so in time it will come up and has to be dealt with. And, as we learn to let go of the fear of death, we experience great liberation for living and expressing as a soul. All religious traditions speak of this liberation and within this arena of soul work this is the final fruit. Figure 6 portrays these levels within the personality.

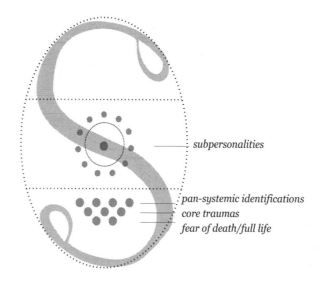

Figure 6
Levels of Personality Structure

Welcome All Experience

It is so important that we do this work with the personality and accept the full range of our personal experience—whatever it has been, and is. In this sense psychological work is spiritual work, for this acceptance allows us to heal and transform the full range of our personal experience so that we are not working against ourselves. I have seen so many "spiritual" individuals and groups ignore this arena and see it as an obstacle to spiritual growth with serious consequences. It is not. Personality work is the needed ground for the soul's force, intent, and qualities in normal life, and we cooperate most fully with our souls by staying very close to this flow of personality experience within us.

The reason for this is that the soul, as I have said, is both guiding the process and is embedded in the experience itself, and complete acceptance of all these layers actually honors the soul and helps release soul force into the world. In this respect you could say that personality is soul and soul personality, even though they are also distinct and usually in conflict. It is important, therefore, to hold that statement as a paradox, for though the soul needs all the personal experience, and "is" this, we, as souls, are also more than our personal experience, as Assagioli reminded me. What is true is that there is one flow of soul force that is either free, or blocked, to some degree, and we work on the personality in order to unblock and free our soul force and increase its expression in the world. The very experience of the personality is where our force is buried, and as the soul process work proceeds in this arena, this vitality is gradually released and we become more fully alive as who we most uniquely are.

A final step that is required is for us eventually to dis-identify from our personalities as a whole. Assagioli explained that to me in our first session. I was identified with my personality and afraid of what I experienced as "above me," my soul. This step starts with dis-identification from subpersonalities, then from the complexes that underlie them in the psyche, then dis-identification from body, feelings, and mind, and only then finally from the personality as a whole. Each step will come when it is time for it, and the key remains to work with what is presented immediately in the soul process.

There are many practices that work with the identification systems of the personality. I want to include one very simple one that is common to these orientations as a representative practice for soul process work in this arena. The exercise that follows is designed to help us work on our personalities from this larger perspective.

PERSONALITY PERSPECTIVE EXERCISE

Sit comfortably in a chair with an empty chair across from you.

Think about the person you were earlier in your life and what the qualities and characteristics of this person were.

Now imagine that person sitting in the chair opposite you. Observe him, or her, carefully, and be aware of the different aspects of his/her experience—some immediately obvious, some more hidden.

Be aware of the complexity of that younger person's life and of his/her struggles as well as gifts.

Be aware of the soul of this person, if you can, and the degree to which it is present, or hidden.

Enter into dialogue with the younger person, as you would a normal conversation, and find out more about his/her experience. Listen to what he/she tells you also.

Be aware of any thoughts, feelings, sensations that you experience as a result of this dialogue and any insights that this perspective on the person that you were bring.

See if you can sense what he/she needs from you, and also what gifts she/he has to give.

Write some about this perspective on one time of your personal life and what you learned from doing this practice.

This same practice can be used in relationship to a subpersonality, a pan-systemic identification, or even the fear of death. It gives us a way to gain perspective on the personality identification system and then to explore what work is needed in order to heal, reorganize, or develop a particular component of the system. The key is to see that whatever arises, deliberately, or spontaneously, is needed in order for the soul process to continue. And over time, as we work in this arena, we gradually transform the personality so that it holds and expresses the force of who we are as souls. Soul and personality then become one, rather than being at odds with each other, and our unique human spiritual maturity is realized in our everyday personal life.

In my own case, this is the work of a lifetime and is not over yet. But I can feel the difference from 30 years ago, and can see the slow progress I have made. Don't be in a rush with this arena, but rather work with it steadily and carefully as it comes. The fruit is worth the long labor.

Arena 3: Psyche

This arena of soul process work holds the unconscious foundations of the personality and its creative and spiritual potential. Assagioli conceived the psyche as an energetic system composed of several dimensions, in which the personality is embedded, and it influences personality through a flow of psychic energy and imagery. Dreams reside in the psyche, and come to consciousness during sleep, but also present are visualizations of myriad sorts that occur spontaneously, or are induced deliberately, while we are awake. The psyche contains a rich storehouse of images and related energies, most of which are unconscious, and which are seeking to come into consciousness as a contribution to soul process. With its images it holds and channels patterned energies that are rooted both in our past and in our future and which represent both blocks and potential to our soul's journey.

Dimensions

The dimensions of the psyche are as follows. I will describe each briefly and then include a diagram (Figure 7) that shows the relationship between them and between psyche and personality. This conception draws directly on Assagioli's work with minor changes.

Present Consciousness: This is the dimension of immediate awareness of experience—our own and others. Within this circle is content of which we are aware moment to moment. The content can be physical, emotional, mental, and can change very quickly, but what distinguishes it is that we are aware of it. That is, it is conscious.

Preconscious: Surrounding this circle of awareness is the dimension of the Preconscious. In this dimension reside images that can be easily called, or recalled, to consciousness, i.e., brought within the circle of present consciousness. Many images reside in this dimension; what typifies them is that they are accessible to our present awareness.

Unconscious: The contents in the unconscious, in contrast to those in the preconscious, are not so immediately accessible to our awareness, but are more deeply unconscious. Those images nearer the surface, so to speak, can be accessible through deliberate visualization, but others that lie deeper in the unconscious will be much harder to reach, if not impossible, at any particular time. At any one point, there will be images/patterns that are totally hidden and unreachable, though they continue to influence our consciousness without our "knowing" it. In time they will come to light, but often not for years, or decades.

Superconscious: The superconscious also holds images that are unconscious, but in a different way from the unconscious. The unconscious holds images of experience that are actual in the sense that they occurred at some point and are buried in this dimension. The superconscious holds images of experience that have yet to happen, potential rather than actual, though we may be quite unaware of them. This potential, in time, comes to light, just as the deep images of the unconscious do, and it can be expressed in personal behavior, but again, it may take years, or decades, for a person to become aware of and fully realize the potential which exists in the superconscious.

Collective Unconscious: This dimension surrounds the psyche—a collective "energy field" with comparable dimensions. Images in this dimension are collective and archetypal, and are linked to, and influence, the contents of the personal psyche. Normally, they do not enter the dimensions of the personal psyche. The idea of the collective unconscious is a major contribution of Carl Jung.

Relationship Between Dimensions

The dotted lines in Figure 7 that make up the boundaries between the dimensions of the psyche represent semipermeable membranes, so to speak, that allow energy to flow between the dimensions, while at the same time maintaining the distinct integrity of each one. When they are too permeable, you can get psychic flooding, and when they

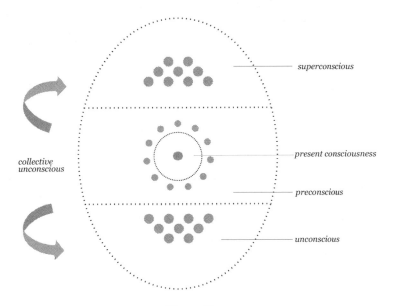

Figure 7
Dimensions of Psyche

are too closed, access to that dimension is closed off and its resources for soul process work are not available. Work in the arena of the psyche includes learning to keep the boundaries at the right degree of permeability and allowing energy to flow through them.

The whole psychical system has its own rhythms and flow of energy, and, just as with the personality, the work involves coming to know just how it operates and to learn to intervene in ways that support its healthy functioning and support of the soul process. We do this little by little, and as we do, a vast resource of experience begins to open to our consciousness and we learn to live within its dimensions in ways that enhance our soul journey.

Pattern

Another way I have come to think about the psyche is that it is composed of dynamic patterns that comprise together a vast, complex, mostly unconscious system for storing, transforming, and channeling psychic energy. These patterns exist in all the dimensions. For example, a personal identification is a pattern of attitudes and behaviors that exists in the preconscious and has roots in patterns that are in the unconscious. An aspect of our potential that is not yet expressed is a pattern of potential in the superconscious. An arche-type, say, of wisdom, is a pattern in the collective unconscious that may have an analogous pattern in the unconscious or superconscious of the psyche.

The soul, which, as I have said, is both guide for the process and embedded in experience, holds a pattern of spiritual maturity (PSM), or wholeness, that is being realized over the course of a life-time. I have come to see the patterns in the psyche as aspects of this potential maturity, and each contributes to it. In soul process work in this arena the soul brings to light those patterns that need to be experienced in consciousness in order for learning to happen and growth to proceed.

Sometimes the pattern emerges from the unconscious in the

form, for example, of early childhood trauma that needs to be made conscious and healed. At another time the pattern might be from the superconscious in the form of an image for a particular quality that we need to own and develop, such as courage or humor. In both cases, as the work proceeds, the learning from that pattern happens and becomes part of our conscious awareness, is grounded in our personal attitudes and behavior, and so contributes to our overall psycho-spiritual development. As the soul process work continues, we become gradually aware of more and more of the patterns, and our consciousness expands into all dimensions of the psyche. This is, in fact, a way of thinking about the emergence of human maturity.

The soul also uses the patterns of the psyche to shape and reshape our personality system towards its fuller expression. What we learn from working with these dimensions affects our personality, and influences and reorganizes it. For example, if a pattern of childhood abuse becomes conscious through regressive work and visualization and the roots of, and reason for, a subpersonality's frightened behavior becomes clear as this trauma is healed, the subpersonality will no longer be as afraid and will be able to behave in new ways. As there is less fear in our personality, for example, another subpersonality, the critical part, is able to relax and not be so immediately on guard, which again will affect our personal life.

As changes happen in the psyche, they affect the personality. Also, as we identify with a new subpersonality and build it in to our personality system, that pattern will in time become unconscious; it will be stored in the unconscious and become automatic. So, for example, if we practice being more courageous and in time build an identification with that quality, we will begin to behave more bravely and eventually, without having to think about it at all, we will simply be brave. We can in this way create and build new patterns that in time will be integrated into the system of the psyche and expressed in our personality. We can develop habits of wholeness.

Gradually, in this way the psyche is transformed and cohered so that it sustains and channels our soul force more consistently, rather than blocking or distorting it. Again, this is work of a lifetime, and the old patterns certainly remain present, but they no longer have the energy stored in them that would influence and affect present behavior. Psyche and personality eventually come to "suit" the soul and can work as instruments of our complex soul awakening.

There are many levels of pattern in the psyche. The most obvious are the biographical, psychodynamic patterns that affect our immediate personal attitudes and behaviors, some conscious, others more unconscious. These include the fear of death and, as we shall see, the fear of being fully alive. But there are other levels as well that in time can emerge and need to be worked with. They include transgenerational patterns, karmic and "past life" patterns, and even pre-birth incarnational patterns that at some point come to light and need to be examined if they are impeding the full expression of the soul.

Beyond these there are patterns in the collective—cultural, national, transcultural—that also influence, and sometimes limit, our soul realization and expression. These are farther reaches of psychic experience that may emerge and need to be dealt with as part of the soul process work. For example, often there can be transgenerational patterns—those that are stored in the unconscious and are passed from generation to generation, for example, the trauma of the Holocaust. There may be cultural and racial patterns that are collective in this more limited sense of the word, which emerge as impediments to psycho-spiritual development. There may also be karmic patterns, often experienced as "past lives" that need to be addressed and transformed in order to grow in this present life. And there can be experiences that do not fit any category, but which emerge and need to be dealt with, for the psyche will bring to light whatever needs to be dealt with in order for the soul process to proceed.

The psyche is vast in all directions, and work with this system takes time and patience. The order of change, however, when it happens, is commensurate with the time it takes, and is immensely fruitful.

IMAGERY EXERCISE

Think of a situation in your life where you feel blocked, or stuck in some pattern that no longer serves you. You want to change it, but cannot. Let the details of this situation fill out in your mind and feelings.

Focus on your body and the physical sensations in it and sense the relationship of these sensations to the thoughts and feelings about the situation.

Now let an image emerge in your mind's eye that is related to the experience of being blocked, or stuck, and the thoughts and feelings associated with it. It may be a literal or a symbolic image, and may include the other senses as well as visual. Let this image fill out in your awareness.

Imagine the image can speak to you and tell you about itself—why it is there, what its meaning is, whatever comes. Listen to the image speak to you and learn what it has to say about the block you are experiencing.

Now let yourself become the image—identify with it—and experience it from the inside, so to speak. See what you learn from doing this.

Become yourself again and hold the image in your mind's eye. Has it changed in any way? How do you see it now?

Let the image fade and pay attention to your experience from doing this exercise. What learning has it brought you? How can you apply this learning to the situation you chose to work on?

Take some notes on this work and ask yourself what the next step is.

The steps of this exercise can be used with any image that emerges from the psyche to learn more about what it is bringing to the light of consciousness. Images from dreams can be worked with in this way, as well as images that emerge when we are awake. They can also be used with images that we evoke deliberately as, for example, superconscious images, and they enable us to establish a relationship with the unconscious flow of energy and imagery that composes the psyche. New images are always emerging from the various dimensions, and as we work with them, we gain a better sense of who we are at that level. We can then work to transform images and release their energy into conscious attitudes and behavior. All this takes time, and is a life work, really, but it is a natural process and in this sense is inevitable, if we are willing to cooperate with it. Once the psyche is resonant it becomes a powerful and steady foundation for the soul's journey. Left to itself, it can undermine and impede the soul's progress, and make the journey much more difficult.

Arena 4: Center

This arena of soul process work is pivotal. It entails the development and strengthening of a center of consciousness, or awareness, in the very middle of the complexity and flow of our human experience. It is a point of consciousness that has no specific content, but rather is a point of presence, or observation, or being, that can be aware of the contents of personality and psyche without becoming identified with them. This point is sometimes referred to as "the fair witness," "the observer" or the "I," and there are many practices from a wide range of disciplines that are focused on finding and developing this human capacity. When we practice presence, we are cultivating this center, and actually when we do the work I have described with personality and psyche, we are also calling on that center as a point of observation of the identifications, images, and energies that are contained in those two systems. The stronger the center, the easier it is to cohere and integrate personality and psyche so that they come in line with the soul. Without it, we can easily lose our way in reactivity and unconsciousness. You can think of the first awakening as the development of this center of consciousness. I depict it in Figure 8.

The center is a psychological point, but it has a spiritual aspect as well. It is the soul at its most particular, the immediate point in our experience through which we can access the soul's being and qualities. It thus serves as a point of psychological integration and spiritual synthesis, and enables the soul to influence and guide the dynamics of the personal and psychical systems. I cannot state strongly enough the importance of the center in the whole endeavor of soul process work. It is the outcome of the first awakening. Without it, we wander; with it, we find our path and stay on it.

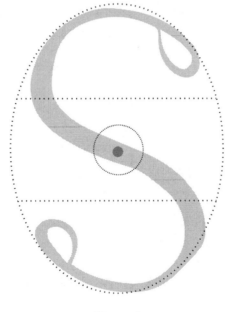

Figure 8
Center and Soul

The core experience of the center is pure being. It is the "is-ness" or "suchness" of human existence, with no particular content, but influencing and organizing all content. It is a resting place in consciousness, a still point, and meditative practices from many traditions are focused on cultivating this point. At the same time, as we shall see, it also has a willing aspect in that from there we are capable of becoming present to, and paying attention to, specific content, and developing an intention over time (sustained presence and attention) that can lead to choices and action.

Assagioli used to say that the center is both being and will, or it is the "will at rest." This is very important, for it means that we can not only get free of old structures and patterns by dis-identifying from them and identifying with the center, or "I"; we can also make choices to build new structures and patterns and give them energy so they grow and replace the old. The cultivation of the center gives us both perspective and power to make changes in our lives, and to gradually align our personality and psyche, or attitudes and behaviors, more directly with ourselves as souls.

CENTER EXERCISE

Here is a classic way of strengthening the center. There are many variations of this exercise, and different terms for the work in different traditions. This one is adapted from Psychosynthesis and I offer it here as a representative practice to discover and build a crucial aspect of soul process work.

This exercise is intended as a tool for achieving the consciousness of the center, or "I," and the ability to focus our attention sequentially on each of our main personality aspects, roles, etc. We then become clearly aware of and can examine their qualities while maintaining the point of view of the observer, and recognizing that the observer is not that which he observes.

In the form that follows, the first phase of the exercise— the dis-identification— consists of three parts dealing with the physical, emotional, and mental aspects of awareness leading to the self-identification phase. Once some experience is gained with it, the exercise can be expanded or modified according to need.

The work builds on Roberto Assagioli's classic "Dis-identification Exercise" and I have both used it in part and amended it in ways that make it more relevant to soul process work. His concept of "dis-identification and self-identification" is a great gift and many schools of psychological thought and practice have now modeled their approaches on it. The Buddhist practice of "Mindfulness" is very kindred and certain forms of Cognitive Behavioral work employ the same dynamic, though the terms used to describe and teach it are different.

Procedure
Put your body in a comfortable and relaxed position and slowly take a few deep breaths. Then make the following affirmation, slowly and thoughtfully: *I have a body and I am more than my body. My body may find itself in different conditions of health or sickness, it may be rested or tired, but that has nothing to do with my self, my real "I." I value my body as my precious instrument of experience and of action in the outer world, but it is only an instrument. I treat it well, I seek to keep it in good health, but it is not myself. I have a body and I am more than my body.*

Now close your eyes, recall briefly in your consciousness the general substance of this affirmation, and then gradually focus your attention on the central concept: "I have a body and I am more than my body." Attempt, as much as you can, to realize this as an experienced fact in your consciousness. Then open your eyes and proceed the same way with the next two stages:

I have emotions and I am more than my emotions. My emotions are diversified, changing, sometimes contradictory. They may swing from love to hatred, from calm to anger, from joy to sorrow, and yet my essence—my true nature—does not change. "I" remain. Though a wave of anger may temporarily submerge me, I know that it will pass in time; therefore I am not this anger. Since I can observe and understand my emotions, and then gradually learn to direct, utilize, and integrate them harmoniously, it is clear that they are not my self. I have emotions and I am more than my emotions.

I have a mind and I am more than my mind. My mind is a valuable tool of discovery and expression, but it is not the essence of my being. Its contents are constantly changing as it embraces new ideas, knowledge, and experience. Sometimes it refuses to obey me. Therefore, it cannot be me, my self. It is an organ of knowledge in regard to both the outer and the inner worlds, but it is not my self. I have a mind and I am more than my mind.

Next comes the phase of identification. Affirm slowly and thoughtfully:

After the dis-identification of myself, the "I," from the contents of consciousness, such as sensations, emotions, thoughts, I recognize and affirm that I am a center of pure self-consciousness. I am a center of will, capable of observing, directing, and using all psychological processes and my physical body.

As our attention is shifted increasingly to the state of "I" consciousness, the identification stage also can be abridged. The goal is to gain enough facility with the exercise so that you can go through each stage of dis-identification swiftly and dynamically in a short time, and then remain in the "I" consciousness for as long as desired. You can then—at will and at any moment— dis-identify from any overpowering emotion, annoying thought, inappropriate role, etc., and from the vantage point of the detached observer gain a clearer understanding of the situation, its meaning, its causes, and the most effective way to deal with it.

Cultivation of the center is pivotal in soul process work and is an essential arena to work in. It enables us both to be aware of and direct the energies of our personal life more creatively and to respond more fully to the presence and guidance of our souls.

Arena 5: Personal Will

This arena has to do with the experience of choice and consequent action and is closely related to the arena of center for two reasons.

The first reason is that the will is rooted in Being and the pure awareness of the center. Will power arises from pure awareness and from the freedom to act, or take no action. The center, thus, is, as I said above, often referred to as "the will at rest." A choice that is connected to the whole being of a person originates in Being, and the challenge is to keep that connection as we move into action. It then serves the needs of the whole person, not just a particular subpersonality.

In order to make this clearer—that the act of will is a process of moving from intention to action—Assagioli broke it down into six steps. I have added three more, as I said in chapter three, to make this origin in Pure Being even more explicit. Roberto's steps are "Intention—Deliberation— Choice—Affirmation—Planning—Direction of the Execution." I have added at the beginning "Being—Presence—Attention." Being is omnidirectional, Presence begins to orient awareness, and Attention makes that focus specific. Then Intention is simply sustained attention over time that leads directly into the Assagioli's six steps. Note that Assagioli calls the last step "direction of the execution," not just action, which implies that the

"I" is still at rest, even as we act, observing the process of choice and the outcome. In a true act of will, we never leave the "I," or center.

The second reason is that choices and action from the center are wise choices, in that they take into account the needs of all the different aspects of the personality and personal life. The center can see the whole and what is truly needed at any moment, and can direct the action accordingly. The problem with the will is that it can get caught in the motives of particular subpersonalities, or complexes, that have their own needs in mind, but not the needs of the whole person. The result is a skewed or flawed choice, which generates reactivity in other parts of the personality, or in the world, and is not quite on the mark. This bias leads to conflict and imbalance and essentially unwise choices and actions, or at least partial and one-sided ones. Conversely, if the will can remain rooted in the center, in Being, then the situation is clearly seen and the needs of the whole person included in the choice and consequent action.

The reason for the steps is that we can break down the act of will and learn where the weak links are between Being and action. Some of us will deliberate for too long and never choose, which means letting go of the other alternatives. Some of us will choose wisely, but fail to affirm the choice with our feelings sufficiently to provide the emotional energy to carry the choice out, or we will fail to plan sufficiently and rush into action in ways that are self-defeating. The skill in using our wills is to stay rooted in Being and at the same time move smoothly through the steps with the whole person in mind, concluding with the direction of the action, or execution.

The soul process work in this arena enables us to strengthen our wills and also gives us increasing power to live as we most want to, and to deal with whatever obstacles are in the way of that more effectively. It gives us the capacity to sense what the potentials are that we want to develop within ourselves, and to design the best ways to actualize those potentials. It also gives us access, so to speak, to our own souls, for the center, as I said earlier, is the soul at its most particular, and from a centered place we can hear more clearly the deeper intentions of our soul and then use the will to carry them out in the world.

The will is, therefore, pivotal in soul process work, and will be required again and again to serve as the agent that is aware and acts on the learning that arises from the experience of the process. Note—this is not the seemingly willful force of a strong subpersonality, or a complex in the personality, driven by unconscious needs. Rather it is the skillful and good will which is seeking a greater aliveness, fuller awareness, and more complete expression. It is a central force in the second and third awakening.

PERSONAL WILL EXERCISE

Pick some area of your life where you would like to make a change, and pick one particular focus for change within that area that would make a difference to you and/or to others.

Sit comfortably and close your eyes and take some time to follow your breathing. Rest in your being.

Gently become aware of the area that you want to work on and become present to the details of the situation without trying to change it, or make any choices. Simply become aware of it.

Begin to let your attention focus on one aspect of the situation that you feel needs change and get a sense of the details of that specific focus. Let your attention rest there and see what more you learn. Study it.

From this formulate an intention to make a change—one that will take attention over time—and express that intention in writing, or to yourself. Hold it in your mind and see if it changes in any way, or holds true. Test it.

Begin to deliberate about all the ways you could carry out this intention, and make sure that you consider lots of possibilities, even some seemingly impractical ones, so you get the full spectrum of potentialities. Write these down so you can review and ponder them.

Take a deep breath and then choose the one that strikes you as the wisest and best choice. See how that choice affects your body as well as feelings and mind. Is there a strong resonance of "yes, that's it"? If so, let go of all the other possibilities and concentrate on that one.

Take time to affirm your choice by imagining the positive and useful consequences and outcomes of making it. Let yourself be excited about the choice and feel how it is the best one for you at this time.

Take time to plan what the next steps are in carrying out your choice and be very specific and practical about it. It is best to plot out small steps that you can take easily, and leave the larger steps until later. Work out a detailed plan to pursue in carrying out the choice, and anticipate some of the resistance you may encounter, both in yourself and from others.

Now take another deep breath and take the first step, whatever it may be, and experience what it brings to you. This is the will in action.

Obviously, this sequence of steps of the act of will can be repeated again and again. Also, if there is a block to one of them, you can go back to that place and work on the block to the flow of energy from Being to action. The act of will is, in fact, one seamless flow of energy, but differentiating the stages allows us to study how well we are making choices and improve how we use our wills. The old adage, "Where there is a will, there's a way" is apt here. And the longer-term work is to gradually align the personal will, arising from the center, with the soul will which I will speak about below, so that the deepest intentions for our life can be grounded and carried out in the everyday world.

Arena 6: Soul Will

This arena of soul work concerns discerning and acting on the intent of the soul for a lifetime—what is sometimes termed the "spiritual will," or soul will—within the context of daily life. We, as souls, are rooted in Being which is experienced most deeply as vitality or force. But this force also has focus and direction; we are here on earth to express who we are fully as well as to be who we most are. In common parlance, the focus is often referred to as the "purpose," "vocation," or "calling," of a particular soul, the direction in life that will yield the most meaning and deepest satisfaction. In the vernacu-

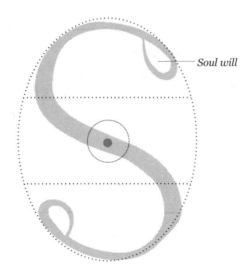

Figure 9
Soul Will

lar, it is "what we are here to do," the path that will lead to the fullest soul realization. The assumption is that each of us is carrying as a soul a particular gift to give, a particular learning that we need in order to mature, and a very particular destiny. We are born with the intent to pursue these, and are "called" to do so, but the circumstances that we encounter, the soul wound that we receive, can impair this capacity.

We can become distracted in any number of ways, and lose touch with this vocation. We settle for less, or for what we think is the best, or what we think is allowed, and then find ways to buffer the secret suffering of loss of soul direction and vocation. We lose our way, quite literally, and wander aimlessly in our living, perhaps being "successful" in terms of family, or culture, but cut off from our deepest intent, and suffering accordingly. Many psychological disorders can be traced to this unacknowledged loss of soul will, and the sorrow of this loss can be very deep.

On the other hand, our soul will is always present; there remains always a secret yearning to respond to and fulfill it. Further, the soul will constantly find ways to remind us of our vocation and to guide us toward its fruition. This often results in a tension between received values— ways of living—and what we know more deeply is right for us. It can also lead to crises wherein our existing meaning system breaks down, offering an opportunity to restore the connection to vocation, or calling, and build a new system and way of living that will enable us to pursue it.

There are also shifts in vocation over the course of a lifetime, so that we can change direction as we grow and mature, and certainly the forms of our soul expression change. Vocation is not a straight line, for it springs from the soul's response to the world as the world changes. But, at root, it is usually a particular gift that does not in essence change, though the forms may shift. Our gift springs from our soul and we are always seeking, even when we are lost, for how we can give it to the world.

Levels of Vocation

Over the years I have come to see that there are three levels of the experience of vocation.

The first is our Being, our sheer presence in the world. This, as I have said, is the core of who we are as souls, and is manifested in the experience of being fully alive.

The second is quality and the manifestation of certain qualities that are differentiations of the soul's force and that qualify its energy. Such qualities flow from the soul into form and can be released, or blocked, according to the conditions of personality, psyche, and body. This level may also contain core values.

The third is form and behavior, which is the most obvious—what the experience of vocation leads to as it is manifested. All three levels are integral to the experience of vocation, but it is important to remember that, even if the vocation is not expressed in behavior, or there is a period where it is not clear what the expression is, the qualities, and soul presence still exist. Fulfillment of vocation entails all three levels. At the moment of death, soul presence remains prime, as it was at birth, and the other two levels become legacy. Our primary purpose is to be who we most are; from this flows the qualities and actions of our gifts to the world.

Soul will does not depend on "doing"; it is in essence "being." In other words, the core of our calling is to be ourselves in essence, not dependent on any particular characteristic or activity. This is what Assagioli means when he speaks of being "a living example." At the same time, we each have gifts to give and the soul process leads naturally to this giving. There is a Hassidic saying that Martin Buber used to share with his students about the soul will. "When you go to Heaven, God will not ask you why you were not Moses. He will ask you why you were not you."

SOUL WILL EXERCISE

Here are three questions that are pertinent to this soul process work with the soul will. Ask yourself each question and take some time to reflect on your answer. Then write the answer down.

> The first question is—What brings you most alive? What are the passions and interests that are closest to who you most are?
>
> The second question is—What distracts you from the pursuit of these passions and interests?
>
> The third question is—Who have been, and are, your allies in this quest?

Now take a moment to think about who have been, or are, allies to your soul. They are most likely people in your life, but they also may be animals, or a particular place in Nature where you have experienced this soul resonance. How have these allies supported you, and do they still, in the expression of your soul will and in dealing with the impediments to this?

With the experience of soul will there is need for discernment and discrimination as to what it actually means for a person. A famous example of this is God's injunction to St. Francis to "Go and rebuild my church." At first Francis thought this meant to rebuild the little ruined church of San Damiano outside the walls of Assisi, and only later did he realize its true import— to rebuild the whole Catholic Church!

Soul will evolves so that the first steps lead to others that we did not imagine, but which follow from the initial actions. A vocation also may change form over time, and yet it can be seen to have the same underlying qualities and intents of the soul, even if the setting and forms are different. For example, a vocation may stay the same in essence and its range of expression expand over a lifetime. It may start in a very local way and then, as we gain experience and skill, the range of expression will grow to national or global, and take on many different forms along the way.

From what you have read of my early life, you can see this struggle clearly, as well as the slow dawning of what I felt I was called to be and do—what my soul will was. I was quite lost in my 20s and it was only with the seemingly accidental reading of Assagioli's book and seeing the oval diagram that I connected directly with my soul will. There had been intimations, and the experience in the church in Florence and the course with Tillich in the two years afterward certainly provided glimpses, but I was unable, because of my own suffering and personality formation, to respond fully. I had a lot to learn and unlearn about myself. Once I found my path, however, the means and range of my soul expression grew dramatically over the following decades, and took many different forms, and is still.

Arena 7: Trauma

It may come as a surprise that the arena of human suffering and trauma is central to soul process work and the process of soul awakening. In spiritual work often there is a tendency to neglect it, or seek to rise above it, or repress and ignore it, but in this approach it is just the opposite: Suffering is the ground that we need to embrace and learn from, for it carries lessons that we deeply need in order to mature and express ourselves fully. The soul process will pass through this arena again and again until we have integrated its profound learning into our daily lives.

This took me a really long time to realize, for I was a child of the '60s, and my early work with myself and with others emphasized transcendence of suffering and experiences of light and love. It was actually my intense suffering in the group in San Francisco that eventually brought me to this realization, and I shifted the focus of

my work to include this arena of experience. "Premature transcendence"—the avoidance of suffering through the misuse of transcendence— still exists in some circles, but in most cases, in spiritual
work, trauma is now included and worked with wisely and directly.

Suffering can arise from the experience of non-welcome that I
described earlier and the soul wound. It can arise from traumatic
physical, emotional, and mental experiences that cannot be integrated and understood by a person, and which proved overwhelming and wounding to the personality, psyche, and will. It can arise
from life conditions and limitations that are no one's doing, but still
impact us painfully. And it can arise from sympathy with the plight
of others and their suffering, both close at hand and around the
world. In this last case, as souls, we are in touch with everything that
is happening, both to us and to others. This sensitivity is often the
source of what feels like personal suffering, but is, in fact, collective.
But we experience it as traumatic.

This is not to say that we would wish suffering on anyone. Quite
the opposite—it is important to work very hard to create conditions
of life that are healing and nourishing for all human beings. But
trying to avoid all suffering is, in fact, impossible. Suffering happens;
trauma happens, and we go on the best we can, creating compensations that allow us to live as well as possible, but always with the
wound inside. What I am saying is, since suffering and trauma exist,
the way to work with them and heal them is to accept and embrace
the experience as something that has come into our lives and that we
can learn from. We would not wish it on anyone, but we can welcome
it as part of our human experience, which is how I finally learned to
deal with the cataclysm of the group in San Francisco.

Again and again, therefore, the soul process will bring our suffering into consciousness in order for it to be known and accepted and
then worked with in any number of ways. This is a central aspect of
our growing as souls on earth. It is not a distraction and not a barrier.
Rather, it is an aspect of human experience that needs to be included

in our consciousness in order to have an experience of the wholeness of Life, and also because it is often directly related to the soul qualities that we are seeking to cultivate and express, and the learning we need to obtain about our own lives. And remember, it contains the descendent aspect of the soul—the embedded soul.

Wound and Gift

What I have come to see over the years is that there is a direct relationship between the wound and the gift of suffering. By this I mean that the suffering we experience is in proportion to the gift we can receive from it and give to the world. Core traumas arise from the wounding of core soul qualities. For example, a person who is very sensitive and tenderhearted is more likely to struggle with fear and anxiety. The person who is angry has the potential for power and good will. The person who is cynical has been wounded in their capacity for faith. I have found that in most cases behind a trauma that leads to suffering there is the potential of a soul quality. Therefore, the suffering needs to be relived and healed so that the quality can be released and expressed. Easy to say, long and hard to do! Certainly there are traumas and suffering that seem intractable and not able to be healed. The work takes time and love, but it is powerful and liberating to think that the suffering we all experience can be transformed and its energy made use of by us, as souls. The challenge is to come to think of suffering as a source of learning that will bring us deeper understanding of the world and the journey we are on. It is as important as any of the other arenas of experience that the soul process brings to consciousness.

Strikingly, in these last 40 years in which the spiritual dimension and the soul have emerged within Psychology, the treatment of trauma has also become a major focus within this same field, and many modalities of trauma work and healing have been developed. They have included many approaches that work with trauma through the body, and it is also interesting to consider that the spectrum of human experience included within Psychology now extends from the physical and neurological to the spiritual. There is a much fuller understanding now of these dimensions of our experience and how we can be wounded.

Thankfully, there are layers of suffering and trauma so that these experiences do not all emerge at once. Rather, the suffering that we can tolerate and work with will come to light and then, as we work with that, the next layer will emerge. Some of the trauma that we have experienced and built our personalities around will not emerge for years, but in time all wounds come to consciousness to be healed and the soul qualities from which they originated expressed.

TRAUMA EXERCISE

Select an area in your life where you are experiencing suffering of some sort. Bring this experience into your consciousness and simply hold it without doing anything about it. Breathe with it and acknowledge it as yours.

Let an image emerge in your mind's eye that is related to the suffering and let it fill out in your imagination. Study it and give it a voice so it can speak to you and tell you more about itself. Be in dialogue with it.

Reflect on what needs to be done to reduce this suffering and heal it, and what the next steps might be. (You can use the steps of the act of will at this point, if that helps.)

Choose a small next step that will relieve your suffering and begin the process of healing and transformation. Imagine what you might experience as you take this step.

Write down what you have learned and what you are going to do.

The soul knows exactly what needs to be done in working with suffering and trauma. It is the personality that shies away, or gets confused, or represses the pain, or whatever. This means two things: 1- Let the soul process bring to you the suffering that needs attention now, and the rest will come in time. 2- Call on your own wisdom to get a sense of the best way to proceed. Certainly consulting others for advice and treatment can be part of this, but in the end it is our own intuition and sense of what is best that is most likely to lead to healing. The point is to learn from the experience of trauma and suffering and let it teach what it knows about Life and about our life. Strangely, given that it has happened, it can become our ally. It is not that we would wish this on ourselves, or anyone, but given it has happened, and is a part of our life experience, the best thing is to embrace and learn from it.

There are many stories of the gift of suffering and trauma, and they are built deeply into the fabric of life on earth. We live in a world where bad and painful things happen, and though we compensate for them as well as we can, and keep going, it is often at great cost. At one point, then, we turn and say, yes, this happened to me and I need to come to know it and embrace it as part of my life. Sometimes this happens spontaneously, sometimes it is through therapy, and usually the turning is preceded by a crisis of some sort that gets our attention and stops us in our compensations, however functional or dysfunctional. The soul work happens, we move through the crisis, learn from it, are changed, and go on, closer to who we most are. And the key in all this is that at some point after that we turn again and say of the suffering, "I am grateful for this and for the crisis it brought me, for I am more myself for it. I would not wish it on anyone, but I have learned from it and am the better for this learning." I can say that now, years later, about my experience in the group in San Francisco.

Arena 8: Soul Qualities

This arena of soul process work concerns the development of specific qualities and ways of being that hold our potential as maturing human beings. They are differentiations of the soul's intent to express (soul will) and exist in the superconscious of the psyche—the dimension that is energetic rather than structural, like the unconscious, and which holds the pattern of the unfolding of the soul process. At any one time we are naturally seeking to develop one or more of these qualities, for we sense that we need them on our journey. There is a listing of common soul qualities later in this chapter. Again, work in this arena involves taking a natural dynamic and making it explicit so that we can cooperate more deliberately with the soul and our deepest intentions.

There are levels of soul qualities. The most immediate are those of which we are aware and desire. They are at the boundary between present consciousness and the superconscious, and by paying close attention to our experience we can discover what quality is to be expressed next more fully. Usually we have an experience of this already, even as we ask the question, and so we can simultaneously look ahead and behind in our experience to identify what is emerging. When we have identified the quality that is new, then we can work to cultivate it, both in the present moment and over time. There are many practices for doing this, but the basic pattern is that we identify the quality, find out as much as we can about it, and then begin to bring it more and more into our daily life through practicing new attitudes and behaviors in our personality.

Of course, there may be blocks to this emergence in our personality and psyche, and so we often need also to uncover and work with these blocks, as well as develop new subpersonalities who can hold and express this quality. Sometimes dream images will indicate the quality that is seeking fuller expression; sometimes we will see it in someone we admire. Whether the source is inner or outer—and usually it is a combination—the work is to identify it precisely and practice making it actual in our life. As we do this, the quality gradually becomes habitual, so that we no longer have to think about being that way, and the pattern drops into the unconscious and becomes a habit we can count on to sustain our soul journey. This takes time and concentration.

Such work brings to light another level of soul qualities that are more deeply stored in the superconscious. They are analogous to the pan-systemic identifications of the unconscious in that they are complex and influence the personality as a whole. If, for example, the quality that is emerging is pan-systemic joy, that joy will flow into many aspects of our lives, not just one. As we work with the immediately emerging discreet qualities needed in one area of our life, those deeper qualities begin to emerge. We work with them in the same way, but their impact is greater on our whole life. The qualities are all aspects of the Pattern of Spiritual Maturity (PSM) that resides in the soul and shapes and guides the maturation of our life.

The deepest level is the core spiritual qualities that we are specifically called to express as souls, and they are usually associated with the experience of vocation. Whereas the other levels are common to all people, the core spiritual qualities will be unique to each of us, for they are the differentiation of the soul's being and carry the unique spiritual DNA. These core qualities are linked to the qualities at the immediate and pan-systemic levels, and work at these levels is essential as preparation for expression of the core qualities that come "straight" from the soul. Just as in the personality we start with

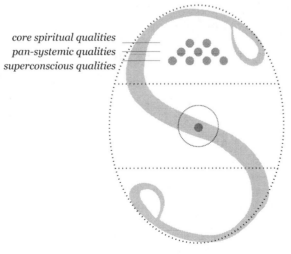

Figure 10
Soul Qualities and Superconscious

subpersonalities, so here we start with the immediate, emerging soul qualities, but the fruit of the work in this arena is the discovery and expression of whom we most are spiritually in qualitative terms. This transcends who we are in quantitative terms (specific identifications) and brings us closer to the essence of who we are as a soul, regardless of what we are doing. For me the quality of Beauty is a core soul quality. For another person it might be Justice, or Truth. I depict these levels in Figure 10.

As I said above, core spiritual qualities often correlate with core traumas—the patterns of which are stored deeply in the unconscious. As we work with either, therefore, the other emerges, and as we shall see, the process of transformation links the two levels powerfully. I have seen this again and again—that out of experiencing a core trauma and working with it, a soul quality will emerge. So, out of rage comes true power; out of grief comes tenderness; out of despair, renewed faith; out of fear, sensitivity. The dynamic of transformation underscores the inherent unity of the soul-personality-psyche-center and the complex process that works these arenas for the benefit of the emergence and maturation of person and soul. The soul process moves where the work is needed, and, under the guidance of the soul, it will move from arena to arena and back again until wholeness is experienced.

Another way to say this is that through soul process our human consciousness expands in all directions, and that present consciousness expands to include more and more of the psyche until its boundaries are contiguous with the entire oval of consciousness. Then all of our experience is contained within the context of the soul. It is a long and complex journey, but we are saved from an overwhelming complexity by the simple and profound practice of returning again and again to the present moment, resting there in the center, experiencing what is emerging, and, in time and space, learning from that. The soul process will bring into the present moment just what is needed for us to proceed on our journey.

SOUL QUALITIES EXERCISE

The purpose of this exercise is to create inner and outer conditions through which we can foster and enhance a desired quality within ourselves. It is suggested for daily practice. In the following outline, the quality of serenity will be used, but the exercise can be adapted for other qualities, such as courage, patience, joy, compassion, etc. It is important that the choice of such a quality and the decision to develop it come from within us, not as a "should," but as something we have chosen purposely and freely as a further step in growth.

Procedure

Assume a state of relaxation and take a few deep breaths. Then think about the idea of serenity: Hold the concept "serenity" in your mind and reflect on it. What is its quality, nature, and meaning?

Open yourself to further ideas or images related to serenity that may emerge from your unconscious and write them down.

Realize the value of serenity, its purpose, its use, especially in our turbulent modern world. Praise serenity in your mind. Desire it.

Assume a physical attitude of serenity. Relax all muscular and nervous tension.

Breathe slowly and rhythmically. Allow serenity to express itself on your face. It may help to visualize yourself with that expression.

Evoke serenity directly. Imagine you are in a place that makes you feel serene: a quiet beach, a temple, a cool green glade, perhaps a place where you have experienced serenity in the past. Try to experience it directly. Repeat the word SERENITY several times. Let serenity permeate you to the point of identification with it, if possible.

Imagine yourself in circumstances common in your daily life which in the past would have tended to upset or irritate you—perhaps being with a hostile person; or facing a difficult problem; or obliged to do many things rapidly; or in danger—and feel yourself calm and serene. (This step may be postponed until you gain some familiarity with the exercise.)

Resolve as much as you can to remain serene throughout the day—to be a living example of serenity, to radiate serenity.

Make a sign with the word SERENITY, using the color and lettering that best conveys this quality to you. Place the sign where you can see it daily and if possible at the time when you need serenity the most. Whenever you look at it recall within yourself the feeling of serenity.

This exercise to develop desired qualities can become the focus of a larger program. You can gather together poetry, symbols, music, drama, artwork, photography, dance, and biographical excerpts, all evoking or in some personal sense symbolizing serenity, and use them for a total experience. By surrounding yourself with these materials, you can evoke and develop a deep sense of serenity—or of any other quality. You can use all that you find in your environment to foster a sense of serenity through your own creation of a synthesis of experiential forms.

A possible contra-indication: In a minority of cases it is possible to experience a negative reaction to the exercise, i.e. attempting to evoke serenity may bring tension, restlessness, anxiety, etc. This is usually a sign that there is an identification that is blocking the development of the desired quality. If the reaction is strong, suspend the use of the exercise and explore what has emerged. After this the exercise can be resumed.

Following are listed common soul qualities that emerge spontaneously and can be cultivated consciously until they become part of our experience.

SOUL QUALITIES

BEAUTY

COMPASSION

COMPREHENSION

COURAGE

CREATIVITY

ENERGY • POWER

ENTHUSIASM

ETERNITY • INFINITY • UNIVERSALITY

FREEDOM • LIBERATION • DETACHMENT

COOPERATION • FRIENDSHIP • BROTHERHOOD

GENEROSITY

GOODNESS

GOODWILL

GRATITUDE • APPRECIATION • ADMIRATION • WONDER

HARMONY • HUMOR • INCLUSIVENESS • JOY • BLISS

LIGHT

LOVE

ORDER

PATIENCE

POSITIVENESS

REALITY • TRUTH • RENEWAL • TRUST • FAITH

SERENITY • PEACE • SERVICE • SILENCE • QUIET • CALM

SIMPLICITY

SYNTHESIS • WHOLENESS

UNDERSTANDING • VITALITY

WILL

WISDOM

These common soul qualities are useful as beginnings in this arena of soul process work, but as we proceed the qualities exhibit unique permutations and combinations, so they become "tailor made" to the particular soul and its unique expression. Again, the best way to discover and work with these qualities within ourselves is to pay very close attention to our experience and what is emerging there. From this examination we will know exactly what quality, or qualities, to cultivate, in what order, and what their relationship is to each other and to us as a soul.

I have worked with men over the years who initially presented an impenetrable personality, and yet, as the work proceeded, it was clear that such an identification was protecting a great deal of sensitivity and fear of being hurt. As this was recognized, they could begin to care for and protect consciously the frightened boy subpersonality, to heal this part, and to cultivate and express the sensitivity directly. They then began to realize that behind the sensitivity was a love of beauty, and that they wanted to bring more beauty into their lives. This in turn brought them great joy. You can see here the relationship between the quality and block, then the deeper quality of sensitivity, and finally the soul quality of beauty. I am one of those men, so I know the territory.

Arena 9: Soul Allies

This arena of soul process work is critical, yet often neglected. We tend to confront our challenges and struggles from a place of separation, and being alone. We forget that all along the way there have been both inner and outer allies to our soul journey. In the Soul Will exercise, you thought about allies who had been there for you in the course of your life journey, and here I want to focus on those allies whom we can evoke and cultivate who are not necessarily from your biographical life. These can include admired historical or religious figures, angels and celestial beings, characters from literature or art, imagined places that we have not been, or mythical animals and beings.

The common factor in these allies is that they resonate with your own soul and they remind you of who you are and what you know as a soul. The contact with an ally can be very powerful and it is always energetic in the sense that there is a spiritual connection between you and this being that springs from a mutual resonance, soul to soul. The form the ally takes is less important than the quality and force of the energy exchanged. You can say that the ally taps and channels the energy of your soul and makes it available to you through its being.

These figures appear, either spontaneously or evoked, and are able to guide and be consulted as to the best way to handle a situation, to make a choice, to affirm a spiritual quality. Wisdom is the usual attribute of a soul ally, but often humor is part of the exchange and also sometimes very practical advice. The soul ally, in resonating with the soul, is holding the whole that the soul sees and so works to right imbalances in the personality and blind spots brought on by identification. The soul ally is always loving and truthful. Occasionally a subpersonality will "dress up" as the ally and try to get its more restricted needs met in this disguise, so again it is really important to sense the quality of the energy that is coming from the soul ally.

Grandparents or trusted friends can sometimes serve this wisdom role, and plants and animals can also serve in this way. And what is most wonderful about this arena of soul work is that people find very particular allies that are precisely suited to their soul and therefore of most help. Over the course of a lifetime, the allies may change, and different ones will emerge at different times and stages. We may have several and evoke them for different purposes. It is all quite particular to each person. At the same time, what happens to all is that gradually we take in the wisdom and make it our own, so that there is less need to evoke a soul ally. The wisdom is ours in any case, and as we work with this arena, we find those allies that are best suited to our soul and come to rely on them, sometimes for decades.

I had a powerful experience with a soul ally when I was in Florence a second time, working with Roberto Assagioli. On my 32nd birthday Roberto suggested that I go walk in the streets of Florence and visit the museums and enjoy the beauty. I went to the Uffizi Gallery and decided to seek out a painting of Christ that would renew the experience I had had years before in Santa Maria Novella. I had no luck and ended up sitting in the very first gallery, exhausted and discouraged. As I was sitting there, dejected, I noticed a small painting of St. Francis by an unknown artist on the opposite wall. I began to focus on the painting and suddenly it was as if it came off the wall toward me and my heart swelled and vibrated with energy and light. My whole body was energized and I realized that this was the painting I was looking for, but it was of St. Francis, not Christ. I rose and walked out of the museum, completely satisfied in my quest. When I told Assagioli about this experience he nodded and said, "So, you have been to see big brother Francis, and it was good." From that moment to now Francis became my soul ally and guide, and saw me through some very hard times on my journey. I realize now that he stepped down the energy of Christ in a way that suited my soul and temperament. He was a lover of animals and the natural world, of poetry and song, and I could identify with him and his life more immediately. He served thus as a conduit for guidance, protection, and love for my soul journey.

I also, much later, had a dog by the name of Taran who was my soul ally for the 15 years of his life, and who accompanied me in the deepest ways through the death of my father and my own dark night of the soul. He found me one day in the woods near where we lived, and 15 years later I held him in my arms as he died. In between we were never apart. Both these soul allies were essential to my journey.

SOUL ALLY EXERCISE

Each of us has within a source of understanding and wisdom that knows who we are, where we have been, and where we are going. It is in tune with our unfolding purpose and senses clearly the next steps to be taken to fulfill this purpose. As we contact it, we can better recognize the difficulties we are having in our growth, and, with its help, can guide our awareness and will toward their resolution. Rightly used, it can help us direct our energies toward achieving increasing integration in our daily living, and toward unifying into one lived reality the personal and spiritual dimensions of our lives.

Many images may be associated with this source of inner guidance. Common ones are the sun, a diamond, a fountain, a star or point of light, an angel, an eagle, dove, or phoenix, the Christ or the Buddha. Different images emerge to meet different needs. However, the one most commonly associated with this source is that of a wise and loving old man or woman. These are two distinct archetypes, with many similarities but also specific differences. It is worthwhile to experiment with both so as to know each well, and know when to use one or the other according to the specific needs of the situation. In general, the wise old man is often encouraging, stimulating, inspiring; the wise old woman is more nurturing, supportive, allowing.

Procedure

This exercise is designed to facilitate contact with one's inner source of wisdom. The simplest procedure is to close your eyes, take a few deep breaths, and then let appear in your imagination the face of a wise old man or woman whose eyes express great love for you. (If you have difficulty in getting an image, you can first imagine a candle flame, burning steadily and quietly, and then let his or her face appear at its very center.)

Engage the figure in dialogue and, in whatever way seems best, use his/her presence and guidance to help you understand better whatever questions, directions, choices, you are dealing with at the moment. (This dialogue may include words, but it may also take place on a non-verbal, visual level of communication and understanding.) Spend as much time as you need in this dialogue, and when you are finished write down what happened, if appropriate, amplifying and evaluating further whatever insights were gained.

After some practice the use of an image may become less necessary, for contact will become steadily more available, perhaps in the form of an inner voice (an example of this would be Socrates' daemon) or simply as a direct knowing of what is the best thing for you to be doing in any given situation. Over time the contact with this soul ally can grow, so that its love and wisdom increasingly can inform and guide our daily lives.

In the use of this exercise, two further mental processes are necessary: discrimination and interpretation. First, we need to learn to discriminate between images that carry true wisdom and those that do not. For example, occasionally a critical and authoritarian figure appears who is not at all loving toward you—the projection of a subpersonality, or a known person, onto the superconscious. Discrimination must be used to recognize it for what it is and "unmask" it. Also, a positive projection onto the superconscious may result in hearing "what you want to," not what is really being communicated.

Secondly, the message received is not always clear in its application and so must be interpreted correctly. As I said earlier, a famous example of this is God's injunction to St. Francis to "Go and rebuild my church." At first Francis thought he was meant to rebuild the little ruined church of San Damiano outside the walls of Assisi, and only later did he realize God wanted him to rebuild the whole Catholic Church!

Thirdly, the soul ally may not be one of these archetypal and common figures, but one quite unique. Yours may not be a being, but rather an animal, or a plant, or even a place on earth that holds special power and wisdom. As you work with this relationship to inner wisdom, you will gradually discover which image is best at making your inherent wisdom available to you. I had a client once whose soul ally was a beautiful island off the coast of Massachusetts.

Fourthly, sometimes there is more than one ally, and these can include living people in your life who have supported you on your journey. Take a moment of silence to express your gratitude to whoever these allies are, and, if it feels right, enter into an imagined conversation with them. You can ask any question you would like, you can listen to what they might say to you, and you can explore with them what can help you take the next steps in pursuing your journey.

Finally, though this contact is important, it is also important not to overuse it. The best procedure is to first explore as fully as possible the dimensions of the problem you are dealing with, and then, when and if you find no solution emerges, ask for guidance.

Arena 10: The Spiritual Adversary

This is a very important arena of soul process work that is often neglected. It is kindred to, though different from, work in the psyche with whatever is unconscious and emerging from the depths, or heights, of that realm. Any aspect of our experience can be unconscious, and, as I have said, the soul process work in the psyche gradually brings more and more to light as consciousness expands to become contiguous with the boundaries of our personal consciousness. These patterns are reworked and enter the unconscious again, but now they are consonant with the soul force and so support our deepest expression. Rather than impeding the soul process, they serve to hold and channel the soul force, and they become, to emend Thomas Merton's "habits of holiness," the "habits of wholeness." This arena of soul process work with the spiritual adversary is different from the above, for it involves an element within us that is spir-itual more than psychological. It is an aspect of our experience that emerges as the soul incarnates and it represents the personal and collective resistance to our soul's intent to express fully our energies, qualities, and gifts on earth in daily life. It is the antipode of the soul will and vocation, and it tests our intent and sharpens it through its very resistance. It is rooted in fear, ignorance, and separation—quite opposite from the soul's love, knowing, and interrelatedness—and can seem to be intentional in its opposition to the soul. In fact, it has no proactive will, but it can have powerful and lethal reactions to steps that we as souls seek to take in a lifetime toward fuller incar-nation and expression. I depict this in Figure 11.

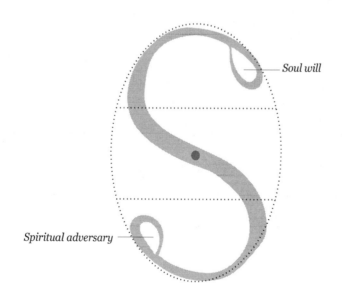

Figure 11
Soul Will and Spiritual Adversary

The term I use for this aspect within us is "the spiritual adversary" and it becomes particularly evident at those choice points where we, as souls, are choosing to go further on our path and take another step toward fulfillment of our vocation. It tends to be quiescent as long as we are following the norms of the culture, or settling for less, though it can torment us about that also at times. When, however, we begin to move on our path in a more deliberate way, and choose beyond our culture and conditioning and for our true selves, the spiritual adversary may come into play. It can be experienced as "inner," or it can be projected on another person, and sometimes it is experienced as both.

We have a number of strategies as the spiritual adversary, when we are identified with it. These include mocking, diminishing, seducing, deceiving, threatening, cruelty, heartlessness, deviousness, rationalization, and many others, all used to stop, or at least distract us from, our soul's path. In most of us this aspect is not dominant, but rather serves as whetstone for the soul, and with awareness and work it can be contained and atrophied. But in some cases we can become identified with the spiritual adversary and stay on the "shadow side" of the soul. If this happens, we not only suffer extreme loss of soul and disconnection, but we can also become a hazard to others on their paths, as in the case of spiritual, or political, leaders who abuse their power to oppress their followers. In common parlance, this aspect is sometimes portrayed as the devil and the battle begins to be framed as one between "good and evil." This oversimplifies the actual situation, however, and leads to projection of the spiritual adversary onto others rather than owning it as an aspect of our experience that we need to confront and deal with ourselves as souls. The work here is much more subtle and concerns identifying the spiritual adversary within ourselves and then examining how it is trying to block and distract us. Once we have a good sense of its "moves," then we can simply ignore it, or counter it with the steps that are best for us as a soul. Through this work gradually its influence will atrophy, but it never disappears. The best way to deal with it is to keep it under our watchful eye and refuse to give it any attention—or give it what I call "benign non-attention."

There is a story that Thich Nhat Hanh tells about the Buddha and the spiritual adversary. In Buddhism the devil is called Mara.

One day Mara is seen approaching the hut in which the Buddha is living. Ananda, the Buddha's chief disciple, is the first to spot Mara approaching and he runs into the meditation hall very upset and calls out to the Buddha "Mara is coming, Mara is coming! What shall we do?" The Buddha calms Ananda and answers, "Why, invite him in for tea. He is our honored guest, for without Mara, there is no Buddha."

This story captures the non-duality, or unity, of the relationship between the soul and the spiritual adversary. The Buddha is very clear about this, but we—Ananda—are not. We panic and become afraid of Mara, which feeds our fear, increases his power, and loosens our connection to our souls and soul will. We want to keep this seemingly malevolent force out of our lives, and so we imagine that it is not in us. We repress and/or project it, or, worse case, express it, which then not only keeps it in our lives unconsciously, but also feeds it psychic energy and encourages it to have more control. Soul connectedness and power reside in our capacity to keep Mara close at hand and under a watchful eye, and even welcome him, as the Buddha did. At the same time we need to choose again and again to give our energy to that which gives Life and strengthens our connection to our soul. And we need to do this despite that very opposition which the adversary provides. We can call on our allies to help us, but key here is the acceptance that Mara, the spiritual adversary, is part of who we are and that the safest place to keep him is in our awareness and close at hand. There is a Cherokee story of an old woman who wore a necklace with two wolf heads on it—one black, one white. When a friend asked, "which one is stronger," she replied, "the one I feed."

SPIRITUAL ADVERSARY EXERCISE

Focus your attention on the darkest parts of your experience, the places that are most destructive to you and to others.

Write about the moments when you have experienced

the presence of this destructive force in you and what happened when you let it take over.

Write about the moments when you experienced this presence and were able to contain its energies and find other ways of responding to the situation.

Write about some of the ways that this element within you tries to sabotage your intentions as a soul. Get a sense for its repertoire of strategies and how you can recognize them.

Have a dialogue with a soul ally about how best to handle this force within you, and what the next steps might be to contain it more effectively without repressing or projecting it.

Write about how this aspect is likely to appear in the future as you move forward on your journey as a soul.

Talk to a trusted friend about this force in you so you make it public and ask your friend about that element within him or her.

This is perhaps the most controversial arena of the ten we have discussed so far in that there are multiple ways you can view this level of experience, and each has advantages and disadvantages. The advantage of naming the energy directly is that often it is not identified, and therefore it operates in the unconscious with impunity or masquerades as a subpersonality. Brought to light, it can be worked with directly and in a different way than a strictly psychological element. The disadvantage is that the spiritual adversary becomes a bogeyman, or devil, that can be easily projected and separated from our immediate experience, which leads to inflation and aggrandizement of the energy and a host of distortions.

For the latter reason it is often safer to correlate this experience with specific psychological trauma and see it as a compensation for extreme trauma, leading to psychopathic and sociopathic attitudes and behavior. It is kept within the psychological realm and treated accordingly. This, indeed, is perhaps the safer route. It has been very useful in my practice, however, sometimes to see this energy directly as the adversary to the soul and to treat it accordingly and in a way different from how I would respond to a psychological entity. Sometimes this is just what is needed, and when it is not named explicitly, I have seen it run amok with its destructive, anti-life energies.

Perhaps it is best to hold both views and to embrace the complexity and the mystery of this force in the psyche. Some people take it very seriously, perhaps too seriously, and others ignore it and dismiss it as medieval. For myself, I see the spiritual adversary as real and active as an antipode to the soul will, and yet I am very open to such dynamics being described and explained in other ways. What is important is that there can be virulent resistance to the soul and the soul's intent, and this can be writ large in groups and nations as well. There seems no other way to adequately understand Hitler and Stalin and many such, or the horrendous atrocities of war. I leave it open to each of us to find the best way to describe and work with this arena of experience. What I have shared above has been my way.

Arena 11: The Body

The physical arena of soul process work is essential to the soul's journey on earth. Our body is not only the vehicle of the soul's incarnation and our instrument of expression, it is potentially the soul itself at its most earthy, or visible. It is the container, or vessel, of the soul. At the beginning of life, at birth, soul and body are close, and people often remark that they can see the soul in the baby—see her essence shining through. We are drawn to infants because we sense the soul nearby and present. Birth is celebrated universally as a sacred moment, and the new body is infused with soul force and new life.

Sadly, in most cases this does not last. Soul and body become separated as the soul wound drives the soul into hiding, so to speak, and the body takes on the tasks of developing in surroundings that do not encourage soul and body to remain close. As we have seen, body, feelings, and mind develop in ways that insure survival and coping with present circumstances, and gradually the personality, grounded in the body, is separated from the soul more and more. Depending on the extent and severity of the soul wound, we will distance ourselves from full bodily experience, even to the point of dissociation or disembodiment, and will lose touch with the sacred ground of physical being. Our body becomes the object that we use and abuse, and all sense of its sacredness, as an aspect of the soul, is lost. Beauty becomes cosmetic, sexuality exploitive, sensuality addictive, and physical prowess exaggerated. The body becomes a buffer to the deeper pain of loss of soul, and, though it sustains our life in the world at a certain level, we remain disconnected from it at a soul level.

It is very striking, as I said earlier, that in the last 30 years, as work with the soul has emerged within Psychology and its presence has been increasingly acknowledged as an important aspect of human experience, the body too has come to be acknowledged as important in healing and personal development. A large number of approaches to the health and healing of the body have developed and increasingly they are being linked to psychological and spiritual health and development. Increasingly the whole spectrum of personal experience—body to soul—is being honored and professionals are more and more sensitive to the interplay and relationship between body, feelings, mind, and spirit.

Behind this shift, I believe, is the growing recognition that the soul is always seeking to restore the connection to the body that was lost because of the soul wound and trauma, and that therefore body work is an important arena of soul work. The intended trajectory of the soul over a lifetime is into full incarnation, so that the personality becomes soul-infused, and the soul force is fully expressed in being and action through the body. "Incarnation" means "in the flesh." Body and soul, thus, become one, as they were at birth—spirit at its most visible—and our bodies come to express fully the soul in the most tangible, physical, and earthy way.

The body, like mind and feelings, can be wounded, and it needs to heal and find those ways of being that resonate with, and carry, the soul force. We develop bad habits, for example, overuse of alcohol, in order to survive and cope, and, as we become more aware of who we most are, we need to work with our bodies to heal and transform them, just as we do with personality and psyche. We need to do this so that they will no longer impede the soul process and can learn to hold and express the full being and energies of the soul. When we talk about the experience of being fully alive, the rapture of being fully alive, this is as much a physical experience as a spiritual one. At those moments body and soul are again one and soul force flows through us unimpeded. Matter and Spirit are one. We all have moments of this union, or reunion, and they become the touchstone for the work we then do on the physical blockages we all have to this experience of full incarnation.

The means to this end are many, and each of us needs to find that form of bodywork that suits our purpose. The body changes slowly and depending on the nature and amount of wounding, this work can take years. But it needs to happen, and spiritual work that disregards this arena is incomplete. Worse, some spiritual systems have demonized the body and encourage people to leave it behind as "sinful," or an impediment to the soul. This keeps us disconnected, not only from the richness of our own physical experience and the enjoyment of Life on earth, but it short-circuits the soul process and blocks full incarnation. We remain dis-incarnate and ungrounded. Without the body, we as souls have no way of fully being here on earth and giving our gift. Right relationship between soul and body is essential to spiritual maturity and soul expression. Kahlil Gibran says in The Prophet, "And the body is the harp of your soul/ And it is yours to bring forth sweet music or confused sounds."

Sexuality is, of course, part of this work and the gamut runs from deeply sensual enjoyment of this procreative and loving energy to abuses of every unimaginable kind, and even entanglement with the energies of the spiritual adversary. This aspect of our bodily experience is clearly part of what we need to examine and come to terms with, both in its strengths and joys, and limitations and sorrows. Sexuality is a central aspect of being human, and each of us needs to discover what it means and how we experience it. The details of this are beyond the scope of this book, but I would only say here that there does exist an experience of sexuality being used as an aspect of the soul's expression and its energies can become aligned with the spirit. In many situations this is not the case, but certainly sexuality can be a powerful means of soul realization and expression.

BODY DIALOGUE EXERCISE

Settle yourself in a quiet and peaceful place and take some time to breathe and rest there.

Close your eyes and scan the experience in your body, starting from your feet and moving slowly and gently up to the very top of your head.

Be aware as fully and with acceptance of what you discover in this scan.

Give your body a voice, based on this experience, and let it speak to you. Ask it what it wants and needs from you, and what the next steps are in meeting these needs.

Ask it how it wants to serve you as a soul and what needs to happen in this regard.

Smile on your body and all its experience. Realize that it is there to learn from and everything can contribute to your journey as a soul.

Experience as much as you can the union of body and soul—that you are, in fact, one, and have only been separated by wounding and circumstances.

Feel the warmth and vitality of your body around you and rest in this. Breathe and feel the soul force flowing in your body.

Summary

These then are some basic guidelines and arenas of soul process work, as I understand it, that we need to come to know in order to support, within ourselves and/or in others, the natural process of soul awakening. The soul process is constantly weaving among these arenas, bringing into the present moment whatever experience needs to be worked with. Our job is to be present to this flow of experience and, gratefully, we are saved from the incomprehensible complexity of the process by being able simply to stay in the present moment and work with immediate experience, trusting that the soul is in there somewhere and is guiding us. In this chapter I have focused on the arenas that bear most immediately on the present moment. In the next chapter I will focus on those that bear on the lifetime, though their effect is always also in the present moment.

In soul process work, it obviously helps to have another person who can witness and facilitate the process as a guide and ally, but, in essence, it is also something that we can do by ourselves, once we understand what is involved. We have the resources to do soul process work on our own, and this is both empowering and enlivening to realize. We are working with something within ourselves that is deeply natural and powerful—an intent to personal wholeness and spiritual maturity—and we, at root, can come to understand it better than anyone else. The soul process remains a miracle and a mystery, and yet at the same time, whether with a guide or on our own, we can also learn to support and nourish it deliberately and skillfully.

FIVE

Soul Process Work: The Lifetime

___

In the last chapter we looked primarily at the arenas of experience that the soul process passes through as it works in our immediate experience. In this chapter we will look at the arenas that are the larger contexts, or containers, for the soul process. The process passes through these also, but over a much greater length of time. They are the larger arenas that contain our experience over a lifetime, and in which we, as souls, seek to awaken and express. The arenas are Birth and the Life Cycle, the Four Awakenings, Crisis, Dying and Death, and Full Life. The chapter ends with consideration of the context of Daily Life and the "Levels of Soul Process," both of which will help integrate the two chapters into one framework. Again, there is a constant interweaving of experience between these two "kinds" of arenas. Present Moment and The Lifetime are inextricably one whole, and yet there is value in making this differentiation, as it gives us a larger view of what is happening in the soul process both in the moment and over time.

Arena 12: Birth and the Life Cycle

This arena of soul process work is the container that holds the others and their interplay in the soul process from birth to death. It is within this context that the soul becomes embodied at birth and then journeys through a series of stages and crises into fuller and fuller awakening, incarnation, and realization. The journey is over at death, and whatever has been experienced and learned is the fruit. Some lives grow richly and deeply throughout the life cycle all by themselves. Most are impaired in a range of ways and need help to make full use of the journey. And some founder and drift to no particular end. But in all cases I have come to hold that all souls intend to travel from birth to death on earth, seeking, knowingly or unknowingly, full aliveness and the realization of who we most are. Therefore, by looking at the life cycle as a whole, and working within it, we can help the soul process happen more easily and fully and come to release our soul force most completely.

The life cycle can be conceived as a series of stages that we pass through. These correlate in part with the bio-psycho-social stages that have been such an important contribution of developmental psychology, but they also have their own spiritual differentiation. Each stage is initiated through a crisis of some sort in which the existing ways in which we have been living break down, either acutely or gradually, and we have to find new ways that are more consonant with our soul. Usually we resist such a change, and for a while there is a struggle between the old and new ways. In time, however, in most cases, the new asserts itself, and we work out a way of living that we discover is even more satisfying to who we are as souls. At each crisis and stage the soul has the opportunity to express more fully, to incarnate more completely, in this life on earth.

Or we could say that we are given the chance at each juncture to become more ourselves than ever. No one welcomes these crises, for we are creatures of habit and they stir the fear of death in our personalities and often feel like dying. But, in retrospect, most will say they are grateful to have had that crisis and to have found their way into a new stage of life, closer to who they most are.

The soul wound can make this process and progression much harder, and the soul hunger can distract us from what will be of most help in this journey. Still, I believe that the natural direction of Life is toward soul awakening, incarnation, and realization, and with more conscious awareness and intent we can make it easier for ourselves and more satisfying. If we can begin to think about our life cycle as a soul journey rather than just a historical developmental progression in time, then we can make choices to enhance the deeper vitality, meaning, and direction, and work deliberately to remove the obstacles to the flow of force and process. We can become midwives to our own souls, and more responsive to the intents and directions that are at the core of our life. We can take our journey on earth more consciously and deliberately. We can hold our ordinary life in this spiritual context and act accordingly day to day.

Note that this perspective on the life cycle is the soul's, not the personality's. The work in this arena is obviously done within the arenas of soul presence—personality—psyche—center— personal will—soul will—trauma—soul qualities—soul allies—spiritual adversary—body. And their interplay within the soul process is described in the previous chapter. The soul work is also done within the arenas of this chapter listed above, but in both the fundamental perspective is from the life of the soul and our learning to see through the soul's eyes.

That is a central tenet of this book. We are souls seeking awakening, incarnation, and realization as human beings on earth, and we experience the life cycle and its challenges and opportunities within this context. This in no way says that traditional developmental thought is not useful—it is completely useful and essential—but the soul perspective does put the life cycle in a new context and allows the soul to be a dynamic aspect of our ordinary human lives. It enables us to think about living as souls on earth from the very beginning of life to the very end. It enables us to work consciously at removing the obstacles to what is, in fact, a natural process that often becomes impeded and blocked, and to make choices that release the being and vitality and qualities of our soul into the world.

Figure 12 represents the stages and crises of the soul journey. It also portrays what I term "the soul line." This represents the path of the soul will and vocation from birth to death and the full expression of the Pattern of Spiritual Maturity (PSM). Ideally, though rarely, we as souls are able to stay on, or close to, it. There are still crises and turning points in the life cycle to be dealt with, some of which are detailed here along the soul line, but if we are able to stay close, or on the soul line, as each crisis emerges and is worked through, we have more soul force available for expression and we realize more of who we most are.

The challenge is that, due to the soul wound, or trauma, or simply enculturation, we as personalities "fall away" from the soul line. I depict this by the wavy line in the lower half of the diagram. These movements away generate soul hunger, which in most cases is then buffered and repressed. At the same time each crisis is an opportunity to move closer to the soul line again, and there is always a hidden tension between personality and soul as long as there is this loss of contact. Often it takes several crises, for there is a degree of "inertia" in the identifications of the personality that are serving our coping and survival. In some cases, where the fear of death, or the soul wound, or the spiritual adversary remain powerful and "weighty," the gap can increase, and this leads to a very different outcome in the life cycle of the person. Yet in most cases, over time, the gap between the personality and the soul line gradually diminishes, as is depicted in the diagram, and soul infusion increases.

The diagram also includes on the upper side above the dotted line the core attributes of the soul force over the span of the life cycle. Within the upper dotted line it includes the four awakenings as well as the presence of Allies and the "I." In the space below the soul line are the obstacles we encounter of all sorts, and below the lower dotted line are the collective forces that counter our soul force and our realization. The spiritual adversary is akin to these and draws on them so I put it just inside the lower dotted line. The one term along the soul line that needs further explanation is "Existential/ Duality Crises." These are crises in the relationship between soul and personality as a whole. In the first, the personality can be quite well integrated, but is cut off from any connection to the soul. In the

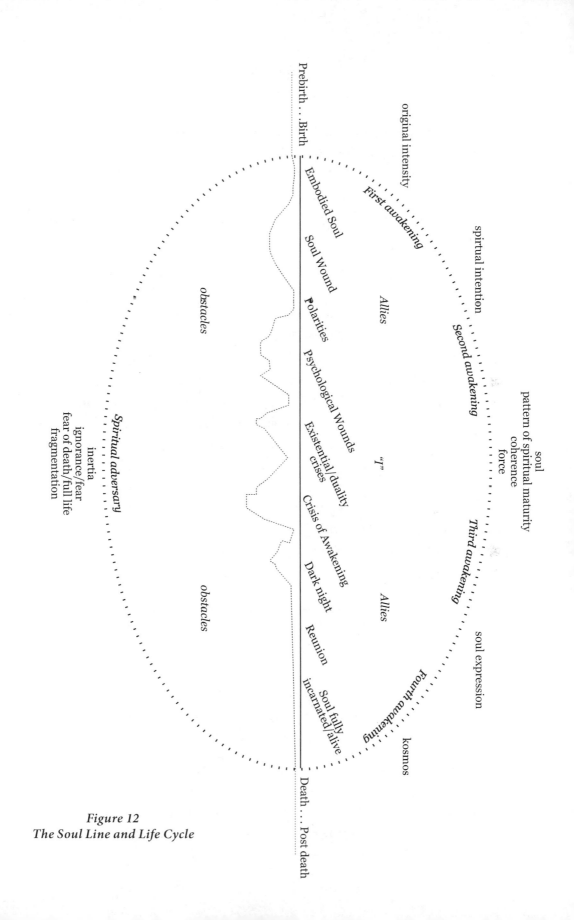

Figure 12
The Soul Line and Life Cycle

second, the personality is "spiritualized" and thinks it is close to the soul, but, in fact, it is trapped in spiritual-seeming identifications and caught in a duality between personality and soul.

Study the diagram and see if you can get a sense of how your life journey is related to what it portrays. Take notes on this learning before you do the next exercise.

LIFE CYCLE REVIEW EXERCISE

This exercise comes in the form of the writing of an autobiography. It may take the form of chapters devoted to different stages of your life, or to crises as markers of significant change in life direction, or any other organizing principle that enables you to look at your life as a whole and gain perspective on the soul journey. It may be that the four awakenings are a frame for this reflection; it may be the series of crises. Ponder on this a while and then write as much or as little as seems useful. Most of all, practice viewing your life as a whole, with numerous stages and phases from this perspective, and see if you can identify the underlying themes, questions and qualities that have been with you over its course.

This exercise is in no way comprehensive—it could not be— but the suggestions may prove to be starting points for the Life Cycle Review. Trust and use what seems best to you to reflect on your life as a whole and the various stages and crises you have been through, as well as what you sense the future holds. Let the writing fit your questions, perspectives, insights, and understandings.

All the stages of the life cycle coexist within us, and under the influence of the soul become more and more harmonious and integrative, so that a human wholeness gradually emerges. The soul process works toward this end and we can cooperate with it so that our life cycle bears out the potential we have been given—one that brings us to a unique experience of personal integration and maturity and a connection with all Life.

When Anne and I went to Florence to study with Assagioli, the first thing he asked us to do was to write an autobiography. Before our first session, he had read these and marked them with mysterious red and blue lines in the margin. Our sense was that he was seeing us as souls in the larger frame of the life cycle and assessing what obstacles and directions would emerge in our soul lives. The depth of his insight into us was certainly aided by these documents and in any case writing them prepared us for being with him and receiving his guidance.

Arena 13: The Four Awakenings

I want to link this perspective on the human life cycle with the four soul awakenings. I presented these in chapter two, and have referred to them several times since, for they are basic to the process of soul awakening. But they bear repeating again, as they are so seminal to this way of conceiving the soul journey over the course of a lifetime.

I deliberately repeat the description of these awakenings in the very words I used before. As you read them again, be aware of how they strike you differently from the first time as a result of what else you have experienced in reading the book.

First Awakening: Self-Awareness

There is a quotation from Jung that says, "Those who look outside, dream; those who look inside, awaken." This "first awakening" in consciousness is to self-awareness, the capacity to be aware of your experience and observe it. It is a skill most human beings gain early in life, and it is supported by most cultures on the planet. In terms I have been using here, it entails the development of the center, or the "I," and increasingly resting there in daily consciousness. There are instances of this not happening, in which case we remain dominated by the unconscious and buffeted by different impulses and unconscious needs, but in evolutionary terms, most of us have mastered this first awakening and are able to be self-reflective and aware of our experience.

Second Awakening: Soul Presence

The "second awakening," as Assagioli was fond of calling it, is one central focus of this book—the growing awareness of ourselves as souls with personalities that are more or less expressive of who we are and the shift of identity from personality to soul. There are many people at work on this second awakening, building on the first, and gaining this perspective in consciousness on their daily life. It is the hallmark and aim of most spiritual practices, and generally it is the fruit of human maturity.

Third Awakening: Soul Incarnation

The "third awakening" is emerging now more and more in people's lives. As I said when I wrote about the principles of transcendence and descendence, as souls we are awakening to the world and our intent to be more deeply incarnated in its ways rather than rising above it. The Boddhisattva within Buddhism is an image of this movement of the soul, as is the Christian emphasis on service— Christ saying, "Feed my sheep!" David Spangler speaks about this as "not being incarnated enough" and "privileging the personal." The direction of soul expression in this awakening is down and in, rather than up and out. Assagioli's emphasis on the will also speaks to the emergence of this third awakening in our human consciousness.

Fourth Awakening: Soul Realization

The "fourth awakening" involves the synthesis of the second and third, and the word "realization" is apt for this, for it can have two meanings—to realize who you are as a soul and to make this real in the world. It also includes a wider realization of who we are in the universe and an experience of total interrelatedness and inter-being with all Life, near and far. The most mature souls have such experience and speak about it in many ways. For most of us, this experience is still ahead. My sense is that the majority of us are at work on the second and third awakenings. There is no reason, however, why more and more people will not come to the realization I describe here, and the species as a whole will mature as a result.

The reason I make these four aspects of the process of soul awakening an arena is that working with the life cycle is an opportunity to assess which awakening is foremost in our experience. Each step is important and rich in experience, and there is no hurry, and still it can help to sense where we are in the sequence. We, as souls, hold within us all four awakenings, but at any particular time we will be largely at work on one. It can be very helpful to get a sense within the life cycle of which is most essential in our own experience and focus there.

At the same time, you may remember that earlier I spoke of the four awakenings as strands in a braided rope, and that the process of how we open to all four is completely unique to each of us, both in timing and in content. Luckily, "our souls know all about it" and the soul process will bring us into the awareness and work we need in the present moment in order to awaken further, whatever that may mean in our lives.

It is possible to extend this frame beyond a single lifetime, so that you could think that one life would be predominately focused on one facet of the process of awakening. Assagioli was fond of saying "A lifetime is a day in the life of the soul." For our purposes, however, I am staying within one life cycle and seeing how we can support our souls to live this given life as fully as possible.

Arena 14: Crisis

There is a well-known Chinese character for "crisis" which translates as "dangerous opportunity." The word "crisis" is derived from the Ancient Greek word for "breaking through" and it implies that some way of living is broken and no longer works. Crises can occur at all levels, and they can be very painful and disorienting. We obviously would prefer that they not occur and yet, strangely, after we have moved through one, and a new life has emerged from the breaking, we often express gratitude for it having happened and for what we learned and what came of the learning. Often we will say that it brought to life a new aspect of ourselves, taught us something new, or brought us closer to who we most are.

Even if the crisis is not catastrophic, but a subtler and more gradual change occurs, we still feel a loss of the old ways. This is true of leaving home, for example, at the end of childhood, or of changing jobs, or partners, as adults, or growing older and needing to retire. Some way of being that we are familiar with no longer works, and we need to let it go and seek out a new way that does. Figure 12 portrays some of the crises that we experience as we develop through the life cycle and take our soul journey. Crises are built into our lives, and change is inevitable. The question is how best to manage these times, and to be open to the good that can come from them. I have found it useful to think of a crisis as having three phases—Resistance/ Letting Go; Not-Knowing, or the In-Between; and Emergence and Integration of the new.

This is a common idea, widely used for both individual and group experiences of crisis, and I have found it very useful in my own life and in working with others. In the terms we have been using here, we could say that we, as souls, seek to make the best use of the inevitable changes in our life. When a crisis happens, we as souls look for the opportunity it provides. The personality, however, resists, and does not want to let go of the old way that is increasingly, or abruptly, broken. Work in the first phase is in helping ourselves let go and accept that this old way is ending.

Then there is the second phase of not knowing, perhaps holy darkness, when it is not at all clear where we are going and who we are. This can be very painful and disorienting, and it also may last a long time. Work here is to learn to bear the unknown and stay close to our experience as it unfolds. We need to learn to live with uncertainty, which can be very hard. Yet people often report experiences of being closer to who they are in essence, even if there is no form. They are in some way relieved to be free of the old way of being, even if they have no idea what lies ahead. Strangely, at such times we often touch this deeper part of our nature, and can begin to see the unknown from that perspective—that as souls we are in the midst of an awakening as well as a dissolution of our old way of living.

Then, at some point, first through glimpses and eventually though an emergence, in the third phase a new way of living takes shape. Whatever we have learned in the Not-Knowing/ In-Between is part of that and also whatever comes to us from our superconscious that is part of the next step in our maturation. This phase can take time, and it is best not to rush, but in fact, to experiment with different ways of being new. Whatever is new also needs to be integrated into our personal lives and take form within our personalities, which also takes time and attention. Work here is to welcome the new and to find ways to bring it into the forms and relationships of our life.

In all this, cultivating the perspective of our souls helps greatly. So does holding the crisis and its phases in a spiritual context as ultimately an opportunity to grow more deeply into whom we most are. Seeking help and guidance often helps, but the wisdom is in each of us as to how to proceed. We just often don't tap it. Remember Assagioli saying to me, "Your soul knows all about it and is only waiting for you to find out." We as souls know our way through a crisis, though we are often not aware of that knowing.

This happened to me when, seemingly out of the blue, I developed Atrial Fibrillation in my heart in the middle of a training institute I was leading in Norway. I was terrified and feared I would die in the next moment. After a night of total panic I found out that the condition was not life-threatening, but the fact that my heart was not as strong as I had counted on it to be was threatening to who I thought I was and how I was living. It was, indeed, a crisis for me.

I returned home and eventually found a way to treat the condition, but the deeper levels of the crisis continued. I felt very vulnerable and not as "strong" as I used to be, and in this condition of infirmity I became very cautious and afraid of doing anything that was strenuous and athletic. I felt I was "no longer the man I used to be" and was for months quite disoriented and confused about what was possible now. I was in the holy darkness.

I discovered, however, during this time that my heart condition brought me closer to myself and other people. I was no longer an invincible leader. I chose to travel much less and stayed close to home, saw my grandchildren more, and experienced much more love in my heart, "wounded" as I was. Eventually in the darkness there were glimmers at first, and then stronger moments, when I felt a new kind of strength coming into me, not heroic and pushing beyond limits, but far more present and tender-hearted. Anne noticed the difference, as did my close friends. And my work with others deepened in some good way.

In the end, I found that I was more myself than before, and more able to be in close touch with others. My physical strength returned to a degree that was viable for my life now, but it was much more supple and relaxed. Looking back, I can see clearly how I, as a soul, opened to the opportunity to express more fully as my physical condition and personal identifications broke down. Could I have known this beforehand? No. I had to pass through the phases of the crisis. But in retrospect, I can see what I had outgrown and needed to change, and how my heart was an active factor to this new way of being which is closer to who I am as a soul. For this I am deeply grateful.

CRISIS EXERCISE

Procedure

This exercise has two parts. The first is to examine a crisis you have already been through, the second to observe one that may be on the horizon still. In both cases the point of the exercise is to look for the phases of crisis and, in the first case, to see how they played out. Then, in the second case, imagine how they might play out, and how you might help with that by taking a soul's eye perspective on what is happening.

Take some time to write about both and be sensitive to what further information and insight comes as you write. Your wisdom may emerge in this self-reflection for both cases of crisis.

We saw this pattern of crisis earlier in my speaking about the principle of transformation in chapter three. We will also see it in the arena of Dying and Death below. It is a very basic pattern by which human consciousness grows and expands to include more and more Life. It can happen in a minute and over a decade, and it teaches us again and again the impermanence of all forms, the presence of the unknown and uncertainty at all times, and the continuous birth of the new. "Behold, I make all things new" is from the Bible, and there are many famous quotations that speak to this basic human experience of crisis and change, death and rebirth, decline and renewal. Here we are seeing it as it underlies the experience of crisis in our lives and can support the further emergence of us as souls.

Arena 15: Dying and Death

This arena of soul process work is central to the whole unfolding of spiritual maturation and the journey of the soul on earth. The awareness of death is what brings us fully alive.

Conversely, it is the fear of death that keeps us from full life. That fear is with us from the beginning of life, and, as I said earlier, serves to keep us alive at the level of survival. But as we proceed on the soul journey, the fear begins to work at cross-purposes to the soul and limits our expression. We hold back, or play it safe, and make choices that seem to offer us security and protection from death. Death becomes the enemy of Life rather than an essential part of it. We seek to buffer ourselves from the fact of death rather than embracing it as a necessary and creative aspect of our life.

The fear of death is rooted deeply in the personality at the boundary between soul and psyche. Close by are the spiritual adversary that can use this fear for its purposes, and the fear of full life, which I will discuss below. In the beginning of the journey we are not directly aware of the fear of death, though it drives development to a large degree, and is always present, if unconscious. However, as we age and move into the second half of life, the sense of mortality begins to emerge as we realize we will not live forever. This awareness is sometimes catalyzed by illness, or other loss, or by the death of parents, spouses, friends and sometimes by the tragic death of our children, and we begin to work out our relationship with dying and death. There is a full range of ways in which we seek to avoid this awareness, and sometimes we can sustain our denial for a while, but eventually we find that we need to accept the fear and deal with it directly.

As souls, we are willing to do this, for we sense that it will take us deeper in incarnation and realization. It is the personality that struggles to overcome the fear and to learn to let go to the fact of death. The earlier work I have described—soul presence, dis-identification from the personality, exploring the psyche, building a center, strengthening the will, discerning soul will and vocation, working with soul qualities, experiencing trauma, finding allies, embracing body as soul ground, and navigating life crises and soul awakenings—all helps. Familiarity with the spiritual adversary keeps it from exploiting this fear for its purpose of distraction. And still it is a long labor, for it entails a fundamental shift of identity from personality to soul, a letting go of all that we cling to in Life and stepping into a place which often at first is experienced as profound emptiness, but eventually can become an unimaginable fullness of gratitude and joy. Not everyone is called to do this, and people progress along that path to varying degrees, but the work in this arena is to come to terms with death as fully as possible and learn to live according to this acceptance.

Death and Rebirth

Luckily, we have a way to practice in this work throughout the life cycle. The principle of transformation is always present, as I said in chapter three, and its core dynamic is constant "death and rebirth." Here we are not dealing with physical death and the end of life, but psychological death, the ending of one way of being in the world, and psychological birth, the beginning of a new way. As we grow and change over the course of the life cycle, as I said above, there are times when an old and familiar way of coping and expressing in the world "dies." We have outgrown it, and, although we may resist this fact for a while, and a crisis often has to break open the system of identification and expression in order to get us to pay attention, in time we let that old way die. Most usually in some form of darkness, we begin to search for the new way that will be more satisfying. "Death and rebirth" is a deep and natural process and rhythm, not only in the human world, but in the natural world also. All of us experience it—whether we know it or not, whether we like it or not—and by becoming aware of it working in us, we prepare ourselves for the coming of physical death and become less afraid. We practice "dying" in accepting change. We experience that beyond this "psychological death" is new life, a rebirth—one that enables us to express even more of who we are. Most meditation practices are rooted in this practice and in the last decades the dynamic of "death and rebirth" as a process in Psychology has become recognized and utilized. In this sense you can say that transformation and death and rebirth within the soul process are the major means that the soul uses to incarnate ever more fully, and when this leads in time to confronting the fear of physical death, we have been prepared to some degree.

The work with dying and death is completely central to soul process work. Without it psycho-spiritual work is superficial and misleading, and fosters forms of human avoidance and immaturity. With it there is the possibility of true human maturity and full incarnation as a soul on earth.

DEATH EXERCISE

Procedure
Sit in a relaxed manner and close your eyes. Concentrate on the rhythm of your breathing and rest in it.

Imagine you are sitting near your own body and that "you" have just died.

Be present to this "you" in this moment of death and be aware of what you experience.

Reflect on the life "you" have led—the experience and learning gained, the core qualities expressed, the fulfillment gained.

Do a life review and take your time with this.

Reflect on what is still undone in your life and what steps are needed to go further and deeper on your soul journey.

Evoke and dialogue with a soul ally about your life, both past and future, and listen to this perspective. If appropriate, ask for guidance and advice.

Let this experience work in you who are alive for a while and be aware of what it brings you.

Continue to breathe and rest and let whatever you have learned sink in.

Open your eyes and take a moment to experience that you are alive and feel the life force coursing through your body and being. Savor the experience.

When you are ready, take some time to write about your experience and learning.

Contact a friend and tell them about the experience and what you learned from it.

Arena 16: Full Life

This arena of soul process work, like that of dying and death, is essential to the soul's journey and the point of it all. It has two aspects. The first is to become aware of, and then cultivate, the moments when we do feel fully and deeply alive as ourselves. Often these moments are fleeting and we miss them, or we devalue them as impractical, or peripheral, to "real" life. We don't pay enough attention to those times when we experience a deep connection, both to our own core, but also to all Life. We don't usually register fully the meaning of these moments and savor them, nor do we then reflect on how these experiences might become more part of our ordinary lives. Rather, we consider them extraordinary and, though we may enjoy them, we do not seek to cultivate them deliberately and shape our living to include this possibility more and more.

When Joseph Campbell spoke to Bill Moyers in their interview about "the rapture of being fully alive," this is what he was talking about. In the terms I am using here I would say these are moments when the soul force pours through personality, psyche, and body and there is an experience both of being who we most are and of being able to express ourselves from this place. It is the point toward which the soul process is leading, and these momentary experiences are forerunners of what is possible in a more sustained way. Abraham Maslow called these moments "peak experiences" and worked to include them within Psychology. In the latter part of his life, after an encounter with his own death, he began to talk about "plateau experiences," which are, to use my words, sustained periods of soul force flow and incarnation. And finally, in the last two years of his life after a major heart attack, he referred to his "post-mortem" life that he experienced, in my terms, as a sustained connection to his soul.

There is no reason why we cannot live in steady touch with who we most are, souls, and express this being and qualities in the ordinary world. This is what I mean by "a fully human life." A full life is available to each and all, provided we are willing to work with the blocks to it that always exist and to cultivate it deliberately. It is where life seeks to move on its own, and as I have said, we can learn to collaborate with this natural process, for our own good and for the good of all. Figure 13 portrays this wholeness of the human being.

The second step concerns working with the fear of full life, which is more subtle, but comparable to the fear of death. Our personal

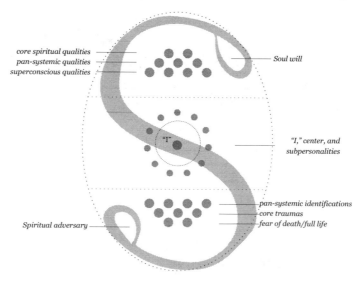

core spiritual qualities
pan-systemic qualities
superconscious qualities

Soul will

"I"

"I," center, and
subpersonalities

pan-systemic identifications
core traumas
fear of death/full life

Spiritual adversary

Figure 13
The Whole Human Being

lives give us security as well as limits, and we often prefer the "cages" we have built for ourselves than full freedom. As the soul process continues, at some point this fear of being fully alive will emerge, because it entails letting go of our more limited identities, opening to the unknown and the boundless, and learning to live as a soul on earth, connected to all other beings, both on earth and beyond. This perspective and spaciousness is frightening to parts of ourselves that are used to more limited forms. We are not at all sure that we really want to let go of everything and dwell in this more expansive world. We prefer our suffering, or our enculturation, or whatever else we are attached to or identified with, and we hold back from the very fullness that we are seeking. Ilio Delia, a Franciscan nun and theologian, refers to this as fear of "the unbearable wholeness of Being."

This aspect of soul process work takes time, and small steps. The fear is deep and is kindred to the fear of death, for both seem to foreshadow dissolution. In fact, as the letting go happens, we begin to realize that everything in our life comes back, but the relationship to these things is completely different. We are no longer attached to an aspect, and so have the freedom to use, or not, anything in service of who we are. It is a great liberation, both from suffering and from limited identity, and in this expansion we discover we have come home to who we have always been. There is a deep familiarity in the experience of full life as well as mystery. We experience the rightness of our particular life and its uniqueness in all aspects and at the same time we feel joined as one with all beings on earth and beyond.

The third step entails learning to bear with grace the intensity of being fully alive. Full life contains the whole spectrum of human experience, including the darkest. Being open to this spectrum means being able to be present to, and hold, not only the most joyous and light-filled experiences, but also the most painful and destructive ones. Human existence is complex and it is not easy to stay in touch with this complexity, which requires being able to welcome the unknown in life and stay open to whatever comes. It means being able to hold all polarities, including birth and death, and not flinch. In order to be able to do this, we need to learn to root and rest in Being and be present to whatever is from there.

The experience of being fully alive as a soul on earth is the experience of spiritual maturity. It entails the healing of the soul wound, engagement with all the arenas of soul work, and expression of the full measure of soul force that resides in each of us. This experience is available to every person and to the species as a whole, as we will see in the next chapter. It is the fruit of the long labor of living and the intention to become who we most are.

It is not an easy journey—in fact, it is a challenging and difficult one—but it is how Life "lives itself more deeply," and, if we are brave enough to begin, Life will come to support us on our way. There are no guarantees, but there is the opportunity to grow and ripen as human beings over the course of a lifetime, to discover and express who we most are, and to make our contribution to the larger world of which we are an indelible part.

FULL LIFE EXERCISE

Procedure

Sit in a relaxed manner and close your eyes. Concentrate on the rhythm of your breathing and rest in it.

Review your life as you have lived it so far and let a moment emerge in your memory when you experienced being fully and deeply alive as yourself.

Relive this moment as fully as possible in your imagination and be aware of the energy and life force that is present in it.

Be aware of the soul qualities present in the moment and any understanding that becomes clear. Also be aware of any fear that you experience of being this alive.

Live this moment as fully as possible now. Let it come into the present. Be aware of how it affects your body, feelings, and mind. Remember to breathe deeply to help bear the intensity.

Evoke and dialogue with a soul ally about that moment and listen to his/her perspective. If appropriate, ask for guidance and advice.

Reflect on how you can bring more such moments into your life in the future, and how you can work with the fear.

Continue to breathe and rest and let whatever you have learned sink in.

Open your eyes when you are ready and take some time to write about your experience and learning.

Daily Life

These, then, are the arenas of experience that I have seen the soul process touch and work in, again and again, within the context of a lifetime. As we engage with them through immediate experience and the present moment, we move to collaborate with our soul in being and intent. We work with the soul process to heal, reorganize, and develop the various aspects of our living so that soul force flows more and more easily and fully, with less constriction, into our daily lives. In this way, through small steps and over time, we come to realize, in both senses of the word, who we truly are. As souls on earth, we awaken fully (see Figure 13).

The process of soul realization is completely natural, as I have said. At the same time there is no surety that this process will unfold into maturity. Each of us has different challenges and opportunities and a lot depends on how we respond to them. We are responsible for our own fate through the awareness that we have and the choices we make based on that awareness. Some choices take us in a particular direction; others can take us in quite the opposite, or into distractions of many sorts. There is no guarantee that life will turn out well for each and all, but there is a lot we can do to affect the outcome.

Again, the key, as I have stated again and again, and as far as I can see, is to stay close to actual experience and to let the soul process work within it. From this living of the experience comes learning and from that understanding and from that choices, but experience needs to remain prime in order for the soul process to work well. Otherwise, if we jump to analysis and understanding prematurely, we begin to work at cross-purposes to the soul. Experience is prime and experiential presence to this flow is essential. This is where the true life is and where the journey happens. Every soul journey is complex and unique, and I believe that each of us has the responsibility and the capacity to live it as well and fully as we can. Not all of us do, but in all cases what needs to be learned is learned and mistakes can always be corrected. The key is to bring the soul's path forward in daily life.

DAILY LIFE EXERCISE

Sit in a relaxed manner and close your eyes. Concentrate on the rhythm of your breathing and rest in it.

Reflect on and hold your life as a whole, as you experience it.

Take some time to cherish this life, to honor its complexities and struggles, its gifts and beauties.

Evoke and dialogue with a soul ally about your whole life and listen to his/her perspective. If appropriate, ask for guidance and advice.

Reflect on the next step in your soul journey and imagine yourself taking this step. Envision the consequences, both immediately and over time. Choose this step.

Open your eyes when you are ready and take some time
to write about your experience and learning.

The sixteen arenas of soul process work described in the previous chapter and in this one have all been focused on the individual:
what the dynamics and issues are in individual experience as well as
how to work with these. And yet it is clear that the individual is in
relationships, not only with significant others, but with family and
friends and strangers and the wider community. Further, the soul
is deeply and widely relational, and connected to others at all levels,
person to planet. As I have said, as we mature as souls we experience
a greater and greater connection with others as well as ourselves and
with all Life. What about these dimensions of our experience?

My answer is that the work starts and ends with each of us,
and without that work, nothing else happens in any steady way.
Conversely, when we take responsibility and begin to examine
our own lives, work to expand and deepen our consciousness, and
express more fully and wisely our values, our relationships with
others change. As we take our place and play our part in the larger
world, it affects our relationships with others, near and far. Of course,
there can be valuable work done in the arenas of relationship and
community, and soul process work leads naturally in these directions.
But too often I have seen the hard work of individual growth and
maturation jumped over in the excitement of relationship, groups,
and community. So I decided, for the purposes of this book, to focus
primarily on the work at the individual level as the *sine qua non* of
spiritual maturity. I am glad to acknowledge that this may be short
sighted and incomplete, because it is, but I have seen enough to know
that the place to start and the place to return again and again is our
own experience and consciousness and how we are growing into the
souls we are. This is how we can change the world.

Levels of Soul Process Work

One more thought that I have found useful for both seeker and practitioner: Think of the working of the soul process as a dynamic nesting hierarchy at the core of which is the present moment. This is the touchstone for all work with it, and we can return again and again to that core and rest there confidently, even when we have no idea what is going on in the process. Around this is the dynamic of movement/resistance moment to moment— that interplay of soul force and inertia out of which will arise the new. From this working out rises the emerging next step in the process, and around this is the experience of a particular phase of life, or a crisis between phases. The larger context for this is the interplay of the facets of the four soul awakenings, and containing all this is the life cycle from birth to death, with its soul line. Then, embracing the life cycle is the soul itself, which is in turn rooted in the eternal and infinite universal Spirit as envisioned in Figure 14.

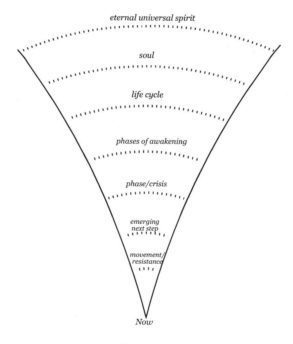

Figure 14
Nesting Soul Process Levels

Think of all these many levels working all the time in a magnificent and mysterious interplay, bringing beauty and complexity to our experience as we move from one to another, or simply rest in the NOW. Everything that is needed for soul process work is in the present moment, provided it is true to what is happening, and at the same time, miraculously, working in the present moment affects the Universal Life we all share. Part and whole are infinitely differentiated and one simultaneously, as depicted in Figure 14.

Sum

In these two detailed chapters I have tried to describe and bring to life some basic guidelines and arenas of soul process work, as I understand it. We need to come to know and work in these in order to support, within ourselves and others, the natural soul process toward soul awakening, incarnation, and realization. As I have said, the soul process is constantly weaving among these arenas, bringing into the present moment whatever experience needs to be worked with. It is one complex process! Gratefully, we are saved from this incomprehensible complexity by being able simply to stay in the present moment and work with immediate experience, trusting that the soul is in there somewhere and is guiding us.

Of course, it helps to have another person who can witness and facilitate the process, and there is a real need for practitioners who have these skills and orientation. But, as I said at the end of the last chapter, it is also something that we can learn to do by ourselves once we understand what is involved. We have the resources to do soul process work on our own, and this is both empowering and enlivening. It is good to know that we are working with something within ourselves that is deeply natural and powerful—an intention and drive to personal wholeness and spiritual maturity. And though it is largely a miracle and a mystery, we can, in fact, learn to support and nourish the process deliberately and skillfully to our own maturity and a better world.

I have also tried to share the details of this approach to soul process work, as I understand it now, so that you, the reader, could enter and explore it. I have not shared everything I have learned over the years, and my learning is still going on, but I hope I have given you enough for you to make a good start and learn the rest by actually doing the work yourself. The key is to get a sense for how you particularly work with the soul process and how this comes through your particular soul and personality. It may be very different from how I would do it, but by taking what is useful and setting out, you will find your own way.

The soul process is mysterious, vital, and beautiful. It is "wild" and cannot be tamed, or predicted, let alone controlled. But we can get close to it, can touch it in ourselves and in others, and learn to be with it more and more intimately. The work of doing this has been a blessing in my life; I hope it will be in yours also.

Daily Bread

Each day I rise, make tea,
Come here and sit.
The dawn is bright, or gray.
I open the gates of Silence.
Listen.
Such sorrow and such beauty
In the world!
I breathe both in,
Breathe out joy.
Above, sun, moon, and stars conspire.
Below, earth births.
Death moves among us,
Winnowing hearts.
My body burns with holy fire.

PART III

Planet

SIX

Soul and Planet

At age 39 I was able to extricate myself and my family from the cult in San Francisco and was instrumental, with others, in bringing it down. A very paranoid residual group left the city under cover of night, and the rest of us looked at each other and began to sort out what had happened. This led in time to some very interesting group leadership work, but at the moment I was devastated, and everything that I had tried to build in my 30s with this group was shattered. The vision was dead, and we were traumatized in ways of which we were not immediately aware. Surely, I was at a new beginning, and I had no idea of where to go, or what to do.

One day I was sitting in our living room and had the experience of a thick fog all around me, filling the space. I felt disconsolate and despairing. I was also paralyzed in terms of acting, though I had made small plans to teach a bit in the next year. On a desk across the room was an earth globe that we had bought for our sons, and through the fog I saw it, and something began to happen. The globe became vivid to me and then, as had Francis in the Uffizi Gallery, it seemed to lift off the desk and come straight at me through the fog. At that moment I heard in my head a voice saying, "Everything from now on that I do has to be in terms of the planet." I was stunned, but the words rang true, and, most amazing, in a flash the fog disappeared and I was flooded with a feeling of peace and recognition of the truth. I understood what my next step would be.

This led in time to helping restore Psychosynthesis in North America in a number of ways in the '80s, to the founding of the Concord Institute in 1990, and the development of Spiritual Psychology. In the '90s it led to training professionals in individual and group work in North America and Europe, to helping a Dutch colleague found a cancer research institute in Rotterdam, Holland, and to co-founding a post-graduate training institute with a group of Russian psychologists in St. Petersburg, Russia. I experienced a powerful flow of creative energy in these various projects and all of them were set in a planetary context. Touchingly, I carried earth flags as gifts to all the places that I taught, and I was constantly speaking about the relationship between individual and group work and the need for the expansion and maturation of the consciousness of the human species, and the recognition of the planet earth as a living system.

Many others were doing this, too. James Lovelock had formulated the "Gaia Hypothesis" and millions of people were at work on the social, economic, political and environmental issues concerning the health and wellbeing of the planet and the species. I was not alone, for sure, but it was a big shift for me, and looking back, I can see it as my version of the third awakening and the call to incarnation as a soul. The group experience had shattered my premature transcendent tendencies, and that day in the living room the desktop globe was calling me in a new direction. Strangely, in time, all the suffering and misguidedness of the group in San Francisco came of use. It taught me what not to do in groups, and how groups, with the best intentions, can go wrong.

In 1989 I had a dream that showed me a pattern of group dynamics, which came to be called the "Corona Process," which demonstrated to me how the soul of a group works through soul process at the group level to build the coherence and health of a group and to shape it into what David Bohm called a "coherent micro-culture." (Bohm, a physicist, posited that this micro-culture serves as a "cell" of peace in the body of the world, and he spent the last years of his life teaching this in an effort to contribute to world peace.) I took that dream and group process into my group work and the teaching of group leadership and was able to seed this way of working with groups in several countries, most particularly Russia. I could not have done so if I had not had the experience in the San Francisco cult.

Person to Planet

From all this I began to posit that the soul process was proceeding on all levels of human organization, and that at every level there was a collective soul that was both guiding the process and embedded in the experience in the same way, though not in the same form, as with the individual. This meant that we could work with the soul process at all these levels—again the forms of work being very different, but pertinent to the level involved—and that there was a correspondence between personal maturity and species maturity. In my own work I had made the link between individual and group work, but others were making the same link at the level of large groups, organizations, subcultures, nations, and the planet as a whole. There were even people thinking about the soul of the planet and the process of realizing the health and vitality of this living system on which all the other levels depended. I recommend the work of Duane Elgin in this regard.

For our purposes here what is important, and what I tried to teach in those years, was that, by working on our own lives in this way, we would also be working on the health and maturity of planetary life. We could make a contribution, both in our own lives and in our work with others. That is what the globe was telling me when it came across the room. The microcosm of our individual life is intimately related to, and embedded in, the life of the planet, and we are responsible for that and for how we live in that planetary context.

Such work on our part is sorely needed. Our human consciousness needs to catch up with the rapid development of technology and globalization. The various crises that we face now on the planet can be seen basically as a result of our immaturity and unconsciousness as a species, even though they take the form of economic, political, social, and environmental crises. Obviously, there are many, many ways of working on the problems we face as a species, and many people are at work on them. But what I want to say here is, let's add work with the soul and soul process to this effort, and realize that the individual consciousness does have an effect on the collective. The planetary crises that we are facing now, seen in this context, can catalyze us to take greater responsibility, to realize that we are not separate from planetary life, but deeply embedded in it, and to do the necessary work to grow ourselves up, i.e. to become the best of who we are—in the parlance I am using here—as souls on earth.

Whole Person/Whole Planet

As we envision and hold the world, so it will come back to us. If we see it as fragmented, it will be in pieces. If we see it as whole and alive, infinitely differentiated and beautiful, then it will come back to us that way. Spiritual and Species Maturity can be conceived as the capacity to experience the inherent interrelatedness of all Life forms on the planet, and the vital force, Life, that enlivens all of us. We can come to this, if we choose to. It is what we, as souls, are doing all the time.

For this reason, and in this spirit, I have titled the book *Holy Fire* and have my painting of the "Fiery Earth" on the cover. I believe that the earth can become the source of its own light in the sense that through soul process work the soul light, or holy fire, in each of us can grow into a spiritual conflagration that becomes species wide. Of course, we cannot be sure this will happen, but we can take responsibility for the maturity of our own consciousness and work with the soul process in ways that move us closer to soul realization. We can decide to take the next step, and the next, following a natural process that is always seeking to guide us. We can all do this.

There is a quotation from the theologian Howard Thurman that I have used in my teaching over the years. He said once in a sermon, "Don't ask what the world needs, ask what brings you most alive, and then go do that, because what the world needs is people who are fully alive." Joseph Campbell would agree.

Soul process work is not only useful for the person, it bears on the planet also, and within the context of our daily lives we have the power to make a contribution at a global level. So often we ask, what can we do? But this we can do, to our benefit and to that of others and the whole world. We need only to conceive that it is possible. To use Assagioli's words, each of us, as a healthy cell in the body of the world, can contribute to "a new civilization, characterized by a harmonious integration and cooperation, pervaded by the spirit of synthesis."

As a case in point, in recent years the effects of climate change and global warming have become increasingly obvious and disruptive. Here is a crisis that is worldwide. Predictably, there is great resistance to acknowledging, let alone doing anything about this crisis, and the costs of this denial mount daily. There is a critical need for us as a species to wake up to this crisis, to grow up and take responsibility for our part in it before it is too late. More and more people are doing this, particularly the young of the next generation, but we are all needed, young and old alike, peoples from all nations and cultures, if we are going to respond creatively and effectively and change drastically our ways of living on the planet. The opportunity is species wide, and the time severely limited. And there is no guarantee we will wake in time.

Yet here too is a tremendous opportunity for our species to change its ways and rise to the challenge presented. We have the capacity, if we take the risks involved, to restore our world and planet and learn to live in ways that sustain rather than destroy Life on earth. And perhaps in this global crisis and in our response a new kind of human being will emerge—one we have not seen before—who will find the ways to live fruitfully and peacefully together on earth. This is possible, and this soul work can play a part in the process of birthing this "new civilization."

A New Self-Interpretation

This brings us back to where I started at the age of 19 with the experience in the church of Santa Maria Novella in Florence and the course with Paul Tillich. Could there be a new version of the human being emerging on the planet, a new "self-interpretation," to use his word for it, that will be characterized by personal wholeness and species maturity? Could it be that we will come to nourish and protect the planet and each other and all beings, and will build up Life rather than destroy it, as we are now? Could it be that we will learn to honor the soul and the natural soul process in ourselves and in others, and, at every level, support the process as it works in all arenas toward the planet's full vitality, beauty, and realization? We are so far from this now that it would be easy to debunk and dismiss the possibility. But think on it and at least hold the question open. It is a vision that is appearing in the minds and hearts of many people in all countries around the globe. Maybe this could happen, and here at least is a way to explore the possibility in our own immediate lives.

Clearly there is urgency to the problems we face as a species, and the litany is long. At the same time, we need only take the next step, whatever it may be, and another will follow from that. I think of Assagioli's aphorism, "Go slow to go fast," applied at the planetary level as well as the personal. In this context we have all the time in the world *and* we need to act. If we can hold this paradox of the soul process, and proceed accordingly, it may be that we can more successfully confront and resolve the issues that trouble us worldwide. And I hear Martin Luther King saying, "We will either learn to live together as brothers and sisters, or we will perish as fools."

Personal Responsibility and Species Maturity

I have come to believe that we each have a personal opportunity and responsibility in this very turbulent time, and in a striking way the fate of the earth depends on what each of us chooses in our individual life. It is so easy to say, "I can't," or "let the others do it," but this is, in fact, a choice to align with the resistance we all have within us also. There is no one out there who will save us; we are the saviors of ourselves, each other, and the planet. Each of us has the capacity to do this soul process work, and there is sufficient support for it once we are willing to take it on. Countless practices exist to help and the soul process itself is only waiting for us to step up in order to lend its support even more fully.

Further, because we are in constant relationship with each other, what we do affects others. How we treat ourselves and others and the planet affects the soul wounding, or soul healing, that occurs as a result. In so many little ways we pass on the collective sorrow of spiritual hunger, or the joy of spiritual connection, in how we think, feel, and act. Either one can spread in a family, or group, or organization, and even from generation to generation. We are far more responsible than we realize, and far more powerful, if we are willing to risk staying true to our experience and learning from it. Species maturation proceeds soul by soul, and there is no other way for each of us, at whatever step we are.

Earth Beauty

I have written about beauty from the very start of this book—the beauty of the human being, the beauty of the soul process—and now I want to speak of the beauty of the earth. Again and again I have seen in my own life, and in the lives of the people I have worked with, that when we slow down enough to fully take in and perceive the beauty of existence on earth, including our own, it takes us toward our soul. When we take in this beauty, receive and appreciate it, it stirs the desire and intent to protect and nourish it, and to contribute to it, at whatever level it exists.

The earth's beauty is a touchstone for the soul and the soul process constantly tends toward the experience of greater and greater capacity to perceive it. In our disconnection and consequent suffering, we become beauty blind, and in our attitudes and actions abuse and neglect the earth. Daily evidence of this violation is so clear. At the same time there are powerful forces in humanity that are seeking to nourish and protect the earth's beauty and to make it more and more present in our lives. I can't tell you the number of clients and friends over the years who have cited beautiful places on earth as havens for their souls and shared experiences of their souls being nourished and strengthened by that beauty. Earth's beauty is the fuel of holy fire.

Planetary Parameters of the Soul Journey

What then are the major parameters of this collective choice to enter in and begin to engage more consciously with the soul journey, the process of awakening, and soul process? This whole book has been a response to that question, but I want to mention several specifics as a way of orienting us to the choice within this planetary context. The soul process work guidelines and arenas of chapters four and five are more specific and psychological, and they are what we can "do," once we begin. These planetary parameters are more existential and frame the context and intent for the specifics of the soul process work at this level. They are the overarching context of the arenas and infuse and support them continually. They comprise a world view that can contain this work and foster it, as well as a place to rest and be while doing it. They are activated and strengthened by conscious choices that we make again and again. They are not given; they are claimed. And when I say "we," I mean the human species as well as the individual. The parameters are as follows:

Presence: This entails the cultivation of presence to whatever experience, inner or outer, exists at any moment and the willingness to be aware of it and study it for what can be learned. It means not turning a "blind eye" to anything, and trusting that every experience has its place and meaning, and is contributing to the journey, even if it is a very difficult or painful one and even if we do not understand how it is contributing. Experience can be from many different levels, from person to planet, but it comes to us in the moment and it is there that we contact it. The choice of presence brings us to the present moment in a way that we can make use of whatever is happening, learn from it, and grow accordingly. Before we can go anywhere, we need to experience exactly where we are.

Potential: This entails the cultivation of our potential, however we experience it. It means living closer to who we most are, and making choices to develop those aspects of ourselves that are part of that identity. Soul qualities and values are central here, and also the choices to act in ways that manifest and express them. Always we have a choice as to what we think and do, and the more awareness we gain, the wiser the choices can be as to how we are and what we do. As our potential becomes increasingly actualized, we become more and more rooted in our own souls and more able to contribute to the world the best of who we are and can be.

Resistance: This entails taking on and studying our own resistance to the soul process flow and how we block and undermine the very thing that we seek. Resistance can take the form of subpersonalities, complexes, or the spiritual adversary; it can take the form of cultural and national limitations, obsolete worldviews, trans-generational patterns, or the fear of death, or of full life. It exists on all levels and is never absent. Without considering resistance and working with it in whatever form it comes, we do not really change. Recognizing and working with it whets the will and also keeps us grounded, for resistance is the very stuff of incarnation and needs to be worked with and transformed in order for the soul force to come through fully. As souls we are able to hold both movement and resistance and study their relationship. As we do this, the whole soul process quickens.

Choice: This entails being willing to choose and take responsibility for who and how we are in the larger world. It means choosing to learn from our experience and to make the needed changes in how we think and feel and act in our lives. It means making our awareness active and real in terms of actual behavior, and accepting that we are, in fact, responsible for our lives, that there is no one to blame, and that, if we are willing to choose and learn to do it well, we can live a fully realized soul life on earth.

Trust: This entails cultivating trust in the soul process and in the unknown that is always part of life and growth. It means developing the capacity to live with, and work with, the unknown, to not be afraid of it, but rather to welcome it and enter into relationship with it in confidence that whatever emerges is just what is needed. The cultivation of trust has to do with a deepening confidence in Life— that it is at root benign—combined with awareness of all aspects of Life, so that we see clearly how to be in the various circumstances in which we find ourselves. It is not "blind trust"; it is awakened trust in the process toward maturity, beauty, and soul realization—one that includes awareness of the whole spectrum of human experience and how complex we truly are.

Faith: This entails choosing to live with the Unknown. It does not spring from knowledge, though knowledge certainly can strengthen faith, but rather from an existential core of accepting and embracing the inherent mystery of Life on earth and the willingness still to live and be and act in our particular lives. Paradoxically, in this choice to welcome uncertainty, if we are able to bear it, we come closer to our souls and are able to live more fully our given life. We gain faith in who we are and in the world. Faith becomes a way to sustain our lives in the face of the Great Unknown.

Place and Part: This entails developing a sense of our particular place and part in Life and discerning how we can contribute to the larger whole of humanity and the earth. Each of us is totally unique, each of us has a gift to give, and each of us has a particular destiny and destination as souls on earth. Gradually, as we proceed on our soul journey, our place and part become clearer. They include both strengths and limitations, and they are very particular to each of us. As we mature, we sense our participation in all Life more and more vividly, but never at the cost of this particularity. It seems we need to learn both to be fully ourselves and, at the same time, one with all Life.

Love: This entails being willing to take the risk of loving ourselves, others, and the world. It means cultivating our capacity to love and removing the obstacles to this loving. It means choosing again and again to cross lines that might separate us from ourselves and each other and to reach to the other, whomever that might be. This does not mean always being "loving," but rather acknowledging that we are inherently joined with one another—all humanity, all species, all beings—and working out how that connection can be affirmed and strengthened. Sometimes this will not look like "love," as in confronting injustice, or inequity, but the root of any action that affirms our inherent interdependence and interconnection within the web of Life is, in essence, love.

Summary

"As the soul goes, so goes the planet." We, as a species, are both problem and solution. The parameters above provide an existential frame for soul process work within a planetary context and the arenas we saw in chapters four and five provide the specific means with which we can do this work. Soul—soul force—soul wound—soul process—soul process work—soul awakening—this is the human soul journey. Each of us has the opportunity to take on this work, and more and more people are doing so each day. We are each alone in this and not alone at all, once we begin. We have everything we need and will discover more along the way, as we need it.

The key is to see opportunity and seize it, to take responsibility for our own life and begin. We can fully claim our lives in this way and take our place on earth. We can find others with whom to share the journey and discover how it is contributing to the larger transformation and development of new ways of living on earth. Everything follows from this choice to begin, and in simply making it we are immediately closer to ourselves and more alive.

SEVEN

Awakening to Kosmos

In my early 60s a strange thing began to happen. One could say that I was at the height of my career, running a busy training institute, teaching in several European countries—including at the graduate training institute I had co-founded in St. Petersburg, Russia—with a full private practice and a reputation in the Boston area for being well versed in the theory and practice of Spiritual Psychology. Yet my interest in all this began to wane, which was confusing and frightening. How could that be happening? I remember announcing my training program for the year 2004-05 and writing in the letter "This will be the last training program." I immediately got scared and changed the letter to say "may be the last," but I could feel that was oppressive to me in some way. I changed it back to "the last" and felt immediately the rightness of this and free. What was going on? I had no idea at first, nor did my colleagues and students. How could I stop now? But I did. In 2005 I ended my training program—and the last year was a stellar one—closed my practice, and Anne and I left Concord and moved to a small farmhouse in the central hills of Massachusetts. I stopped traveling to Europe and Russia to teach, largely stayed home, and in time descended into what I recognized eventually as a "dark night of the soul," or what I call in this book "holy darkness."

This was a profoundly disorienting development, and to deal with it I sought help from a Jungian analyst who had been a Carmelite monk for 30 years before he took up this therapeutic work. This was new territory for me, and I was scared. I will always remember what he said to me in our first session: "Tom, it all has to go." This terrified me and yet I also realized that it was true in some way that I did not understand and that I was in just the right place.

The work was largely with my dreams, which had many archetypal elements, and with the gradual systematic dismantling of the structures of my personality and psyche that I had come to count on and use quite well in my life and work during my 40s and 50s. As they dissolved, there was an experience of deepening darkness and of not knowing who I was anymore, and the sensation of being stripped gradually and systematically of every personal identification through which I had come to know myself over the past decades. It felt like a total annihilation, or crucifixion, of my personality, which left me very vulnerable, almost like a newborn.

At the same time I also experienced the deep support of my own soul as well as Anne's, this therapist's, my sons' and their families, and a few close friends, and this kept me going. In fact, I found myself closer to them than ever before and far more open to their love and care for me. It seemed I was both dying and being born at the same time into some new being, and this was all mixed in my daily living. The experience was profoundly disorienting and frightening, but what I learned to do eventually was to simply stay with whatever was happening and trust that it was for a reason and there was something for me to learn from it. That steadied me in the darkness and I learned to breathe and be with whatever came.

Now, looking back, I would say that during my "dark night" I experienced a shattering of some major ideas that I had held about myself. One was that I was very alone. I had always been a secret loner, though a charming one, and the experience in the cult in San Francisco reinforced that perception. Yet gradually in this darkness I began to experience that I was not alone and isolated at all, but rather closely joined with my family and friends and with the world as a whole. Something was holding me that I had not been able to feel before, and it was joining me with all Life.

Another idea was that I was a hero, a champion of certain ideas, and so somewhat above the plane of normal life, with its pains and sorrows. My heroism took the form of idealism and optimism, and had been the foundation of the work that I had done in the last three decades. Yet this too was shattered and I experienced more and more my vulnerability as a human being. My life was ordinary, and fragile, and painful, in the present and in the past. This was overwhelming at first, and, in turn, brought levels of anxiety to the surface of which I was not previously aware. Yet in time I came to accept that those feelings were mine and true, that I was still "here," and that I could experience them and survive.

A third idea was that I was special, that I was in some way better than most, a cut above the rest, which set me apart from others in a more privileged position in life. This was partly from my family, partly from my education, partly from my background, and though I exercised "noblesse oblige" and put my talents into good works, my hidden sense of difference and elevation was still there. In the holy darkness it became very clear that this was not the case at all, and that I was simply one of an infinite number of human beings on the planet who were seeking to survive and thrive on earth. I was humbled and leveled in quite an absolute way. One of so many!

This shattering of ideas of myself was devastating, but also liberating; in the end, it brought me more into balance within myself and with Life. The process of getting older was a factor, and also some physical ailments, so I was confronted with my waning prowess and power as the man I thought I was. There was great fear and sadness in this realization and, at the same time, strange to say, relief. I could also feel in the darkness that someone new was emerging and I got glimpses of him, both in my dreams and in how I experienced my actual life. Living in the country contributed to this emergence, as did discovering a new community. It provided strangeness initially, but eventually new ways of being presented themselves, like having a large garden, getting to know neighboring farmers, and having clear access to the moon and stars at night.

I continued to do my work during my "dark night" in a limited way, mostly with a small practice, but also with some teaching with a small group of students. Both were rich and vital, though I was often exhausted at the end of a day. The Big Work, however, was gone, stripped away, and who I had been in those decades was dead. I lost all clear sense of who I was, with only the conviction that my soul was still close and faith that something new would come of this. I struggled with my vulnerability and hypersensitivity, and was humbled and constantly amazed and grateful for the people around me. I could feel their love. I had no sense, however, of where I was going, for I had lost all that I had known myself to be. Strange to say, I had the experience of being no-one in the sense that all my personal identifications had melted, or been striped away, and I was totally "in the dark" about who I was now. At the same time I experienced being very alive, very close to Life, embedded in It, and in this sense deeply connected to everything that was alive—from my family and friends to the sun, moon, and stars. I found myself, indeed, in intimate relation to Everyone/Everything. It was as if I was widely aware of Life, so I did not feel abandoned, and yet I was no-one other than an alive human being, empty and full at the same time.

My holy darkness lasted a long time—years—but slowly I did begin to feel a strength returning that was entirely different from the old one, and a tender sensitivity to a fuller range of human experience and existence that I had not had before. I had the sense of being born anew, and coming into a new phase of my life quite different from the previous ones. And yet I was still myself at the core, more myself really, and this was strange at first, as if I had both changed dramatically and not changed at all in the depths of my being.

My emergence also came in cycles, not as a line, and even as I was feeling better and stronger, a deeper level of anxiety emerged and I found a trauma therapist who used EMDR and worked intensively to unlock some of the still unintegrated traumas of my life, particularly around the experience in San Francisco. Through this therapy I got to the root of the despair I had been avoiding all my life and, amazingly, as I was willing to experience this and stay with it, the anxiety largely disappeared. It seemed that the anxiety had been a buffer to this deeper experience of despair, and as it diminished, I began to experience a new vitality and deep joy in being alive and a profound connection to all living beings and the planet as a whole. My outer life had not changed much, except for aging, but inside it was all quite new.

New Being

Little by little I began to write and paint again, to teach a bit more, and to expand my practice, but it was all quite different now; I was a different man whom I had to get to know. It is so hard to describe, but gradually there was a renewal of life in me that has continued to this day, and a growing experience of joy and gratitude in simply being alive. It was so much more simple, really, and yet at the same time I became much more able to embrace complexity and uncertainty, to bear sorrow, suffering, and even despair, my own and others', and to live in the moment as it came. I would say now that, from this experience of holy darkness, I have become much closer to my soul and who I most am as a person. From here I can look back over my life and see my soul journey in its stages and turning points, and this is certainly another. The term I often used in my journal writing during this time was "ripening." Nothing was being added, much had fallen away, and yet I was experiencing a ripening, a maturing, of who I was in the world, a fuller sense of who I am. Out of the darkness everything came back, but in a different way. There were no additions, just more of me. So hard to express!

This process is nowhere near over, but I can say now that I experienced in those years a passage in my mature life through a deep darkness, a total loss of who I had been, and then a slow birth of myself into a new life. I think of T. S. Eliot's lines in the *Four Quartets*:

> *We shall not cease from exploration*
> *And the end of all our exploring*
> *Will be to arrive where we started*
> *And know the place for the first time.*

The experience I have more now is one of paradox and of the inherent complexity of Life and its incredible enduring beauty. Where I will go from here is unknown, except that I will at some point die. But for the moment I can say that I am deeply, deeply grateful to be alive.

Awakening to Kosmos

Throughout this book we have seen how the process of soul awakening moves through the first, second, and third awakenings. Now, as we end, I want to say a bit more about how it moves us into the fourth awakening—one that is truly mysterious and which contains and synthesizes the other three. I have called this awakening soul realization, using the word in both meanings of, one, the reality of the soul's existence, and two, making the soul real in our lives through presence, values, meaning, and expression. And I have also referred to the fourth awakening as a realization of "kosmos."

In these last years I have tried to find a way of speaking about the experience of full awakening, incarnation, and participation in the living universe as a soul and as a very particular whole human being, and I have found that the term "kosmos" comes closest. "Kosmos" is a word from Ancient Greek—a very apt and beautiful word in that language, because it means both "immediate beauty," and "beauty of the whole." It is, thus, both microcosmic and macrocosmic beauty. Further, it also means "deep and natural order"—and it points to the existence of a deep natural order to the world, to the universe, one that is not random, or mechanical, but inherent and organic to

Life. This is the way Pythagoras used the word in his teaching—to mean at the same time beauty and deep order, both of the microcosm and the macrocosm. The word "cosmetic" is derived from it, but it is a degradation of the term, denoting superficial beauty, for in its original meaning, kosmos points to the inherent deep beauty of all people and beings, and to the beauty of the earth and the Universe. In this original meaning beauty and deep order are one.

When we are deeply connected to Life as a soul—when we've awakened as a soul, when soul and personality are integrated in the way I've talked about here, and when we are becoming more fully incarnated and realized as souls—I believe we have an increasing experience of "kosmos." We experience our own particular place, part, and being in the world which brings us a sense of our own beauty and the deep order of our life and connection with all others. We also experience an immediate apperception of how incredibly beautiful the world is, in both senses of the word, and the beauty and order of a Universe that is alive and holy. As we awaken as souls, we increasingly have this apperception of beauty near and far—almost as if this is how we as souls were seeing the world all the time. This is the experience of "kosmos," and the core of the fourth awakening.

Conversely, in our more limited and identified consciousness, in our wounds and reactions, we fragment this apperception of "kosmos." In our suffering and our inability to stay connected, we cannot sustain it, and it comes to us only in glimpses that are soon lost. In this respect, we are still largely beauty blind as a species. At the same time, as we have seen, as we proceed on our journeys, and awaken, mature, and manifest who we truly are, we uncover this capacity in ourselves to experience kosmos. We discover it is a birthright we can claim and make our own. We increasingly and consistently behold the beauty and deep order of the world and universe, and we experience ourselves as part of this, along with all other beings. Consequently, as I have said earlier, we choose increasingly to celebrate and protect this Life rather than exploit and destroy it.

Kosmos springs from our growing capacity to embrace complexity and paradox and to realize that the Heaven, or Paradise, or Afterlife, that we have projected is, in fact, right here now before our very eyes. And once we begin to see the world in this way, we can never go back to destroying it and each other as we are now.

Kosmos and Seamless Reality

Sometimes in spiritual, religious, and philosophical thinking, there occurs a split between material and non-material reality, or between form and formlessness. Often too there arises from this a hierarchical differentiation whereby the spiritual formlessness is considered "higher" than the material/formal levels, and therefore more pure and valuable. Religious teachings have definitely contributed to this split, as did Plato and Aristotle, each in his own way—one with the perfect ideas beyond form, and the other with the objectification of matter by detached observation.

With the experience of kosmos I am suggesting something quite different. In the experience of kosmos there is no such split. Rather there is the paradoxical experience of Life force both holding and infusing all forms of reality while at the same time being embedded in them, so that there is only one seamless living reality infinitely differentiated. Paradoxically, Existence is Spirit, Spirit is Existence; there is no split.

This Seamless Reality is in no way monolithic, but rather incredibly and infinitely diverse, constantly changing and in process, incomplete, and, at the same coherent and deeply orderly. In this reality the world is holy, and that holiness is totally in the world, not apart from it. The Universe and everything in it is alive and holy, but at no loss to the incredible uniqueness of each being. In fact, this perspective enables each being to be more itself while participating at the same time in the holy web of Life.

I have come to believe that for us on earth there is nowhere else to go, there is no other place where perfection lies. Rather, everything is right here. Of course, there is the soul process and change and transformation, and the details of this are what this book is about. But the context for these is a seamless reality of Life that includes birth and death, which is forever now, and always growing and changing.

As we awaken as souls, and particularly in the fourth awakening, it seems to me that we begin to experience that All Life is literally one, interrelated whole, at no loss of the infinite differentiation of the myriad forms. This is a paradox that we learn to bear and embrace in our consciousness and in our living. It is a way of speaking about spiritual maturity and the fruitfulness of the long soul journey. It is an experience that we have all touched at some point, and all secretly yearn for. And yet, to "get there" we need only pay attention to where we are, no matter where that is, and be present to the soul path of our immediate experience.

Again, this experience of kosmos includes the complexity, uncertainty, and unknown of human existence as well as the deep order and beauty I speak about above. It also includes the imperfection and unfinished development of human beings, the inherent suffering of life on earth, and the open and still unrealized future that we all face. Yet all this is held in a new way. We can become capable of embracing it from a place in our consciousness that is able to hold, and bear, it all. Somehow it too is part and parcel of our human existence and contributes to the beauty and mystery we perceive.

The fourth awakening leads to the experience of kosmos and seamless reality. This experience can come to any individual and is the core of what may eventually emerge on the planet as species maturity and a consequent new way of living on earth. The process of soul awakening moves in this direction and soul process work can be one of an infinite number of ways to support it.

Kosmos and Emptiness

Paradoxically, kosmos is rooted in the experience of emptiness, of no-thing, for it emerges when we have let go of every identification that is partial and would distract us from the Whole of Life. Fullness and emptiness become one in kosmos, and we have the experience of being deeply who we are and at the same time being no-one. We lose ourselves completely in order to be fully ourselves, and we need to let go of all of who we are in order for all this to come back to us without identification with it. Thomas Merton describes it this way: "At the center of our being is a point of nothingness—it is like a pure diamond, blazing with the invisible light of Heaven. It is in everybody and if we could see it we would see these billions of points of light coming together in the face and blaze of a sun that would make all darkness and cruelty of life vanish completely."

In my terms this is the conflagration of holy fire that I saw in my dream, and in the period of my holy darkness I sense I touched this experience.

Kosmos and Silence

Assagioli once said to me, " Silence is the language of Being." In chapter six I talked about a group falling silent in the presence of the collective soul force among them, and in the Appendix I speak to practitioners of silence as "the most powerful intervention you can make." I think of Shakespeare's Cordelia and her response to King Lear's question of how much each of his daughters loved him—"Love and be silent." Hers turns out to be the truest love.

Silence is the doorway to the soul, and in spiritual practice, east and west, it is the centerpiece. In the terms I am using here silence is the ground of Experiential Presence and evokes the soul force field that then quickens the soul process. Silence is both the first and the last step to Kosmos, in which all the opposites are synthesized and the beauty and deep order of the soul shines through.

Our being is by nature silent, and as we learn to live more and more from this center of consciousness as souls, our words and actions increasingly arise from this still source within us. It is in our silent being that we become most connected to who we truly are.

Kosmos and Love

As we have seen, at its core the fourth awakening is kosmos and Being, and the miracle of this experience is that from here springs love. This is not a love that is limited to one as opposed to another. Rather it is love for all beings and creatures and the earth itself springing from the realization of being a living part of the Whole of Life. It is the natural fruition of the process of soul awakening, and it comes to us in deep and quiet ways—a love for ourselves as well as others—and with a deep kindredness with all Life.

So much has been said about love over the centuries that I will not say more, but will only assert here that the fourth awakening and the experience of kosmos do not leave us alone, but rather loving and beloved as the very human beings we are. It is the love that Dante refers to at the end of *The Divine Comedy* as "the love that moves the sun and stars"—the love that is the birthright of all human beings and which we seek, knowingly and unknowingly, to find and express in "our ever mortal lives."

Kosmos and Holy Fire

In the dream with which this book began I had a vision of sparks of white fire in every cell of my body that were resonant with the light of the stars. I called this "holy fire" and connected it to the presence of soul force within each cell. We have seen in this book how holy fire is the very being and vitality that works through the soul process toward soul awakening and expression, and we have followed the course of that process in many different ways.

Now we are relating it to the experience of kosmos and to the beauty and deep order of Life and the Universe. It turns out that holy fire is at the heart of the soul and of kosmos, and as we awaken, we burn more and more fully and brightly with it. It becomes the beauty we are and the expanding light of our consciousness. It is both our essence and our existence, the force of our soul on earth, our radiance. It is mysterious and "wild" as I have said, and does not submit itself to easy understanding or control. But I believe it is the birthright of all beings and can grow among us so that the earth becomes a source of soul light and we illumine the world and everyday life with our holy fire.

Our Human Future

Clearly, we are at a critical point in our evolution as a species. The world as we have known it is breaking down—some say dying. Its living systems are collapsing, or degenerating, we are racked with problems and turmoil at all levels, and the inequities within the species are increasing. We are living beyond our means as a species and stressing the earth systems beyond their capacity to sustain us, let alone the other species with whom we share the planet. Globalization and technological innovation have revolutionized our communication and interdependence as a species, but they have brought with them a host of problems for which at the moment we have no solution. From this perspective the future looks bleak, and there is growing fear that the chaos will engulf us and render the planet a wasteland.

At the same time there are signs everywhere of renewal and new approaches to the troubles we face, and a new generation maturing who are holding their lives in new ways, very different from the presently dominant worldviews. We have seen in countless individual lives that out of chaos, suffering, and disintegration can come new ways of being that are vastly more satisfying and creative, and there is no reason not to think that this too could be true of the planet and the species now. Of course, there is no telling, but certainly the potential and possibility exists and many, many people are working toward this outcome. We live in tumultuous times and the future is unknown.

In the terms of this book, I would say again that a key to our coming through this critical period and having Life continue on earth in some enriching way is the development and maturation of human consciousness and the consequent attitudes and behavior that spring from this burgeoning. We understand enough to know that this maturation of the human being is possible and desirable, and that it is built into us in a natural way that we can learn to trust and support. In this book I have attempted to give a sense of how this might happen, and how it is happening.

No doubt this is only one among the many ways that this will come about. There may be a fifth awakening in store for us, there may be a series of crises that will galvanize the species in unexpected ways, or there may be a cosmic crisis that will finally awaken us to who and where we are. Time will tell.

Whatever the case, we do know that we have a future in common, that we are indelibly interdependent and interrelated, and that we will share the fate of the earth, whatever it is. We also know that we can work to expand and transform our consciousness, that there are ways to do this, and that we are not alone in seeking these means. And we know, right in the present moment, that the Beauty of the earth, of the Universe, and of ourselves and all beings is evident, if we open our eyes and hearts and minds to it. We live in a world that is beautiful beyond belief, and we know as souls we are capable of perceiving this and acting to protect and sustain it. The future is far from hopeless, and is full of possibility. We need only begin and keep going. We need only to, in the words of my youth, "Stay bare and seek."

AFTERWORD

The quest of my life, as you now know, has been to try to understand the spiritual nature of human beings and to learn as much as I could about the human soul. This search has led me into many inner and outer places and into the work of many people. And what understanding I have has risen from both my own experience as well as from that of people I have worked with over the years as a guide and teacher. I had no idea, when I set out, that this would be my fate, but in looking back, I can see how well it fit me, and I am grateful for it.

On this journey I have come to believe that each of us has a particular soul calling and journey, each of us has struggles and obstacles to overcome, and each of us has the potential for a full human aliveness and expression. Life itself tends in these directions, and, at the same time, we can embrace this calling and journey more consciously, and work deliberately and cooperatively with the process of awakening, incarnation, and realization as souls and our maturation as human beings. This is my response to the question I asked at age 19 in the church of Santa Maria Novella and the fruit of the quest that followed for now almost 60 years. It has been my life and this book is a report on that soul journey—one that is not yet over and in which I still pursue both question and quest.

Holy Fire has enabled me to pull together my thoughts and feelings about this work with the soul and soul process and to share them with you. They are incomplete, but they represent the best I have from my quest and my question. I am so grateful to have had the opportunity to pursue this question and to have the life I have had as a result. I am so grateful to have known the people I do and shared my search with them over all these years, and this includes my dear family and friends as well as teachers, colleagues, and students. All have been a profound blessing to me. I can't imagine living any other life now, though certainly it has not been an easy one, and there have been moments when I would have traded it for any other.

Invitation

And so, in ending, I invite you, dear reader and fellow traveler, to use whatever is useful here for your own journey, and I encourage you to respond to your own questions and quest in ways that suit your soul. I believe that each of us has the possibility and the capacity to live fully our given lives and to pursue the quests and questions that have the most meaning to us. In this we are alone, and at the same time in good company, both from those who have done this before us and those who are traveling with us now. Most of all, we are in good company with our own souls, for, as we proceed, we burn more and more brightly with holy fire and can find our way more easily in the dark. We realize we are part of something much larger and wiser, and that we are held in love as we journey. The world becomes holy before our eyes and the universe alive around us.

So, wherever in the world you are, in whatever place on the planet, I extend great good wishes to you and blessings. May we awaken, each and all, in time and space, and find our soul's way home!

APPENDIX

A SHORT NOTE TO PRACTITIONERS

I want to make a few comments to the practitioner who might want to use this approach in professional work with others. These points are incomplete, but are basic to this orientation, and they may be useful to those of you who are working with others.

The first is that this work goes best with others when you are doing it yourself in your own life. There is no such thing as standing apart at an analytical distance and doing soul work from there. You need to know the territory first hand as well as possible, and then your help will have life to it, and you will be given everything you need in order to do it well.

The second point is to be aware of the shift in power between you and the soul of the client, or friend, in this way of working. You are no longer the expert in what needs to happen, the person is, and you are there to help that knowing emerge. We are used to being in charge as professionals, or parents, and take pride in our competence, but here we need to learn also to let go and accord power and dignity to the client, or child, and the soul, the power who is guiding the process, and who knows better than we how to proceed. The knowing may be hidden and need help to be revealed, but the basic orientation here is that the person is the authority on her/his life, not you.

The third point is to take small steps in the work. The soul process proceeds by small steps and in this way leaves nothing out, but sometimes in our excitement we can try to leap ahead and push for more to happen than is ready to. This creates a subtle distraction in the flow, and the person is torn between staying with what is in the moment or jumping ahead to a conclusion, or whatever. There is a timing to the flow of experience that is best supported by small steps and being in no hurry.

This is also true of the "shape of the session." The soul process will quicken and work, as I have described, and then at some point it will slow and come to ground. If we push at that point for more work to happen, it aborts the natural timing of the process. "Less is more" here, for then there is time to integrate the learning from the experience before going on to the next. Small steps are best.

The fourth point concerns interventions. Think of your silent experiential presence as the most powerful intervention that you can make. This energizes the soul force field as nothing else can.

The next most powerful intervention is what I call an "open" intervention. "What are you experiencing now?" "Stay with that," "Allow that experience," "See what happens next," are all examples. They do not add anything to the soul process; they only amplify what is already happening.

The third most powerful intervention is what I call "directive," when you ask a person to do something such as "Let an image emerge for the feeling you are having." You are adding something here, which only works if it does not disrupt the process, but enhances it. If a directive intervention works, the person won't even notice it. It is like a template that you place alongside the process to support its flow. If it does not work, and interrupts the process, then the soul field will wane, and the person will be forced to choose between the natural process and complying with our well-intentioned, but misguided, intervention.

The fifth point is to hold the soul process work as imperfect and unfinished, rather than complete and done at any point. This keeps the whole endeavor open and alive, partly known, partly unknown, and always changing. The Buddhist idea of "Impermanence" is useful here, and, paradoxically, this attitude enhances the power and effectiveness of the process rather than limiting it. Life itself is largely unknown, and we live better when we "leave a little room for the Mystery." So it is also with soul process work; holding it this way aligns it with Life and enables it to work more fully within us.

⌒

CODA: THE APHORISMS OF ROBERTO ASSAGIOLI

I want to share one more perspective on the soul process work that brings us around to Roberto Assagioli again. It comes in the form of his favorite aphorisms that he used again and again in his work with me and others. They are catchy guidelines that are easily remembered and applied, and come with his characteristic mix of humor and wisdom. I have used them throughout my work as a teacher and therapist/ guide, and want to include them here, both because they are so useful and also to honor him. They will be familiar to you from what I have said earlier in other ways, and perhaps more memorable.

"Go slow to go fast" or "Make Haste Slowly"

This is the central paradox of soul process work, encouraging us to not miss a step and to stay close to the natural f low of experience in the present moment. By doing this, which may seem slower, we, in fact, move faster, because we are in sync with the soul.

"Work under the Aspect of Eternity"

Here he evokes the perspective of the soul who is partly beyond time and space and is bringing this context to the personal work and soul process. There is no hurry and, in fact, nowhere to go but here now, which is the doorway to Eternity. This experience of the Now/ Eternal is central to soul process work, as we have seen.

"For one person, one thing; for another, quite the opposite"

Here is a marvelous emphasis on the complete uniqueness of each person and what they need at any particular point. There is no orthodoxy, or one size fits all, but rather a deep respect and attention paid to the individual and what each of us needs in order to grow and mature.

"Never either/or; always both/and"

Here is the paradox of polarity and the potential for the "balance and synthesis of opposites"—a favorite topic of Roberto's. It supports the complexity of soul process and the unknown in it as it works in our experience. Polarization impedes the process; this attitude nurtures it.

"You are perfectly imperfect"

Here is the affirmation of the unknown and imperfect, again in the form of a paradox, so that human perfection is possible in its very imperfection and humanity. "What a relief!" He would say, and I hear myself sighing to this day when I hear it again.

"Your soul knows all about it; is only waiting for you to find out"

This is familiar from earlier in the book, but what is radical about it is that it affirms our reality as souls—this is who we are—and at the same time we are working and awakening to find out who we are, so that the paradox holds and we remain one being, soul and human being.

"There is no security, only adventure"

Here he is speaking to the tendency of our personalities to cling to safety of various kinds while the soul in us is adventurous and comfortable with the unknown. He is affirming the mystery of the soul process and encouraging us to enter fully into the adventure of life. He said this when he was in his 80s.

"Be a living example"

Here he is speaking to the process of incarnation as a soul and embodying our consciousness in our daily life. This is more important than anything special we might do, or think we need to do. It is our life itself that counts most.

"Leave a little room for the Mystery"

Here is a favorite of mine, which I have cited again and again in my own life and in my teaching. It was said to me with a touch of humor and affectionate irony, knowing it would be hard for me, and at the same time compelling. Both have been true.

"We must learn to live as souls on earth"

Here is the whole endeavor in a nutshell, including the four awakenings and the vicissitudes of the soul process within the context of life on earth. It is the task that we all share, knowingly or unknowingly, and, according to how we progress, we will contribute to the overall maturity of the species and the health of the planet.

ENDNOTES

ACKNOWLEDGMENTS

How to acknowledge those who have helped and accompanied me along the way? It seems impossible, given how many and varied the people are, how rich the company.

On the professional side, over the years I have been blessed with the presence and company of fine teachers, colleagues, and students who saw and encouraged in me qualities I was not sure of about myself. They helped me see more clearly who I was and where I wanted to go with my work, and then left me free to pursue it, and often accompanied me along the way.

On the personal side, I have had deep friendships over the decades in North America, Europe, and Russia that grew out of my work and became a brother/sisterhood in shared life and vision. This community has lasted long, and, having started out young, we now are sharing the processes of aging and death. I was lonely as a child, and suffered from this, but in the end I can see that I have been richly befriended and have great company to keep.

On the familial side, my mother and father got me started and sustained my soul in the first decades of my life, and then I met my wife, Anne, who more than anyone has been a trusted and beloved partner in deep life for more than 50 years. Our sons, Peter and

Benjamin, gave us the great gift of being our sons, and more recently in their marriages, marvelous daughters-in-law, Kate and Kristin, and grandchildren—Ada, Josiah, Levi, Landon, and Ethan. My marriage and family have been very central to my life, and learning to love these dear people, and be loved in return, has taught me much that I needed to know. I have loved being a husband, father, and now grandfather, and the richness of this family life has infused and sustained my professional work immeasurably.

I want also to acknowledge the readers I asked to give me feedback on this manuscript. Rich Borofsky, Yoav Dattilo, Piero Ferrucci, Penny Gill, Louisa Mattson, Chelsea Wakefield, Hedi Weiler, Bryan Wittine, and Joe Landon all read it carefully and made comments, large and small, that helped me twist the lens of the work to greater clarity and depth. Piero also graciously agreed to write the Foreword. And my deep gratitude goes to Maureen Moore for her tireless help in putting this manuscript together and publishing it, and to Ellen Eller for her sharp eye and great skill as a copy editor.

Anne, my wife and life partner, also read the manuscript and gave me detailed and very valuable feedback. She has believed in, and supported, my work over many decades in countless ways, tangible and intangible. In her I found a soul companion, and I treasure the journey of our shared life.

And last, but not least, I want to acknowledge my own soul, which has guided and sustained me in all manner of difficulties, challenges, and accomplishments, and has brought me a deep experience of the beauty of Life and the resilience to live it fully. Without this source of deep life, I would have been lost. I have been blessed on my own life journey, and this book is a small return for all that has been given along the way by people near and far, old and young, who loved me and stood by me to share the journey. Setting out, I did not believe this possible. It is only now, as I look back over the decades, that I can see the richness of the human company I have kept and that kept me, and I am amazed and grateful.

SEMINAL INFLUENCES

This selective listing of my influences includes the works that have been seminal in my thinking and experience. These works span a range of genres, including the arts, for it is through them all that I have come to the ideas and experiences contained in this book. I offer this in lieu of a comprehensive accounting of available resources in the field of Spirituality and Psychology, as these are myriad and increasing every day and readily available. This is the work that influenced me most deeply and changed my life.

Psychological Work

Roberto Assagioli
Carl Jung
Stanislav Grof
Frederick Perls
John Firman/Ann Gila
Erik Erikson
James F.T. Bugental
Abraham Maslow
Carl Rogers

Religious/Philosophical Work

Ralph Waldo Emerson, The Essays and Journals
Henry David Thoreau, particularly *Walden*
Paul Tillich, particularly *The Courage to Be*
Thomas Merton, particularly *The Inner Experience*
Martin Buber, particularly *I-Thou*
C. S. Lewis, particularly *The Screwtape Letters*
Suzuki Roshi, particularly *Zen Mind, Beginner's Mind*
Thich Na Hanh

Spiritual Work

Joseph Campbell
Joanna Macy
Thomas Berry, particularly *The Great Work*

Duane Elgin, particularly *The Living Universe*
Karlfried Graf Durkheim, particularly *The Way of Transformation*

Literary Work
Sophocles, particularly *The Theban Trilogy*
William Shakespeare, particularly *King Lear and the History Plays*
Leo Tolstoy, particularly *Anna Karenina*
Fyodor Dostoyevsky, particularly *The Brothers Karamazov*
Boris Pasternak, the poetry and fiction particularly *Dr. Zhivago*
D.H. Lawrence, the poetry and novels particularly *Sons and Lovers*

Poetic Work
T. S. Eliot, particularly *The Four Quartets*
Rainer Maria Rilke, particularly *The Duino Elegies*
Dylan Thomas
George Seferis
Thomas Merton
Walt Whitman
 W.S. Merwin
Mary Oliver

Artistic Work
Vincent Van Gogh
Claude Monet
Paul Gauguin
Georgia O'Keefe
the German Fauves

ABOUT THE AUTHOR

Thomas Yeomans, Ph.D. is the founder and director of the Concord Institute and co-founder, with Russian colleagues, of the International School, a post-graduate training institute in St. Petersburg, Russia. His background includes education at Harvard, Oxford, and the University of California, and professional work in the fields of literature, education, and psychology. Since 1970 he has worked as a psychotherapist, teacher, and trainer of professionals in Psychosynthesis and Spiritual Psychology throughout North America and in Europe and Russia.

He has published writing on Psychosynthesis and Spiritual Psychology, as well as three volumes of poetry and a children's book. He is also a painter and musician. Currently he maintains a private practice in soul process guiding/mentoring and teaches occasional training seminars in Soul Process Work.

He lives with his wife, Anne, in a small farmhouse with a large garden on a hillside in Western Massachusetts.

The light which puts out our eyes is darkness to us.
Only that day dawns to which we are awake.
There is more day to dawn. The sun is but a morning star.

—last lines of Henry David Thoreau's *Walden*

More Praise for *Holy Fire*

A powerful statement and at the same time a practical guide for deep psychotherapy, it leads you to the darkest regions of the psyche and the highest peaks of the human spirit in a clear and skillful way.

—Piero Ferrucci (Italy), psychotherapist, and author of
The Power of Kindness, Beauty and the Soul,
Your Inner Will and other books.

How fortunate we are that Tom Yeomans, spiritual teacher, clinician, and poet, has gifted us with this profound work, born of his big heart, brilliant mind, and amplitude of soul. Written for spiritual seekers of all traditions, his model outlines a pathway through the complexities of living fully on this earth while remaining connected and directed by the magnificent and mysterious power of the Soul. He writes with a "voice" that conveys warmth and wisdom, as if we are sitting with him, as he guides us through the dimensions, distractions and difficulties of living soulfully on earth. In section two, he outlines explorations and practices by which we can deepen our confidence and connection with the guidance of soul, and heal the access to our own deep wisdom and become more confident and trusting that our soul is always guiding, even through the dark passages of our lives.

—Chelsea Wakefield, Ph.D., (USA) Associate Professor of Psychiatry,
University of Arkansas for Medical Sciences.
Author of *Negotiating the Inner Peace Treaty*,
and *The Labyrinth of Love*

This wonderful book by Tom Yeomans is a luminous and exemplary application of the guiding principle of all the theory and practice of Psychosynthesis: the principle of integration, organization, and synthesis. This is a very important and current point in this world characterized by increasing complexity at all levels. Further, Tom manages to reconcile the paradox within Psychosynthesis (with all the risks involved if the right balance is lost) between the drive for evolution and living in the present moment. This is a milestone. Human evolution takes place precisely through an ever deeper rooting in the present moment and in an ever fuller acceptance of reality, exactly as it is moment by moment.

—Petra Guggisberg Nocelli, (Switzerland), psychotherapist, trainer and author of *The Way of Psychosynthesis* and *Know, Master, and Transform Yourself*

Over the past 35 years, I've witnessed the extraordinary power of Tom Yeomans' teaching and therapeutic work. In *Holy Fire: The Process of Soul Awakening,* he shares his visionary understanding of the soul, along with a wealth of practical strategies for nurturing its development. He also shares an intimate glimpse into his own soul's journey, allowing us to accompany him through the inspiration and the challenges that informed his evolving vision. *Holy Fire* is a rare treasure to be opened by anyone—therapist, counselor, educator, sincere seeker—who is serious about exploring the nature of the soul and its evolution.

—Jeffrey Rossman, Ph.D. (USA), Director of Life Management, Canyon Ranch and author of *The Mind-Body Mood Solution*.

Holy Fire shares the transformative wisdom gleaned from a lifetime devoted to living the highest ideals and plumbing our inner depths. It is the record and gift of a life well lived which encourages and enables us to live more deeply, sensitively, and soulfully.

Roger Walsh MD, PhD. (USA) Professor of Psychiatry, University of California, Irvine Author of *Essential Spirituality*

Tom Yeomans' book, *Holy fire: The Process of Soul Awakening,* is a gift that can be unwrapped over and over again. It offers both a place to rest and a call for action. I have known Tom for a lifetime, and his qualities of professional and personal authority, generosity and acceptance comes through in this book. The balance of speaking clearly, leading the way, and at the same time inviting the reader to find his or her own voice, and be true to his or her own path, is captured in this book. Tom's writing is infused with a basic trust in the individual's own wisdom and strength, and at the same time his writing offers support and encouragement based in deeply rooted wisdom and shared life experience. This bold book can be used as a solid source for teaching and guiding others, and if we do so, its wisdom speaks most clearly through our own personal encounter with the book as we live what we teach. Reading this book is like being on a journey and seeing both the landscape and the map for the first time, but knowing you have been here before. Tom's book is a gentle, but firm nudge; Keep on walking, you are not alone.

—Liv Grendstad Rousseau,(Norway)
Associate Professor in Counseling Education
Department of Education, University of Agder, Norway

Tom Yeomans' *Holy Fire: The Process of Soul Awakening* is an inspired integration of his multi-dimensional lifetime experience as a teacher, therapist, artist, and explorer within the fields of Spirituality and Psychology. When I read the book originally, I wrote this.

I find myself caught up in an energetic vortex of thought, feeling, and sensation and I luxuriate in it. It's a visceral experience to read the definitions, ponder the ideas, and do the practices. Everything flows so naturally, logically and deeply, warmly and beautifully.

This statement still captures my experience with subsequent readings. Always there is a sense that Soul is speaking.

—Hedwig Weiler, MSN, (USA) Founder of the
Psychosynthesis Center of Wisconsin.

Made in the USA
Columbia, SC
12 March 2020